COMMUNITY DEVELOPMENT AND CIVIL SOCIETY

Making connections in the European context

Paul Henderson and Ilona Vercseg

This edition published in Great Britain in 2010 by

The Policy Press
University of Bristol
Fourth Floor
Beacon House
Queen's Road
Bristol BS8 1QU
UK

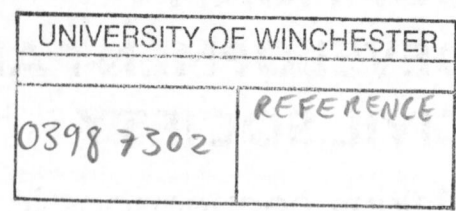

Tel +44 (0)117 331 4054
Fax +44 (0)117 331 4093
e-mail tpp-info@bristol.ac.uk
www.policypress.co.uk

North American office:
The Policy Press
c/o International Specialized Books Services (ISBS)
920 NE 58th Avenue, Suite 300
Portland, OR 97213-3786, USA
Tel +1 503 287 3093
Fax +1 503 280 8832
e-mail info@isbs.com

British Library Cataloguing in Publication Data
A catalogue record for this book is available from the British Library.

Library of Congress Cataloging-in-Publication Data
A catalog record for this book has been requested.

ISBN 978 1 86134 969 9 paperback
ISBN 978 1 86134 970 5 hardcover

The right of Paul Henderson and Ilona Vercseg to be identified as authors of this
work has been asserted by them in accordance with the 1988 Copyright, Designs
and Patents Act.

Cover design by Qube Design Associates, Bristol
Front cover: image kindly supplied by www.istock.com
Printed and bound in Great Britain by TJ International, Padstow

For Barbara Henderson and Tamás A. Varga

Contents

Foreword

At first glance Paul Henderson and Ilona Vercseg's book might be taken as one 'on community and civil society'. A more perceptive observer might add 'European' as an important qualification. Upon a deeper reading, however, it will become obvious that this is not just a book on community and civil society in Europe. The piece in the reader's hands is a product of civil society and community practice of *European* significance.

Realising this makes the work a lot more worth exploring, and not only for the initiated community practitioner. In fact, referring to it as a 'product' does not do justice to the nature of the achievement. Albeit in a professedly 'modest and personal' way, the volume makes available a veritable harvest of several decades of sustained effort in national and European-level community building, and spells out its relevance for civil societies.

Put in this perspective, the wealth of the experience encapsulated within the text's confines is nothing short of arresting. When writing a 'foreword' to the authors' output, one cannot but recall how improbable such an outcome looked like from Hungary in the 1970s when the first attempts were made in that 'other part' of Europe at charting how the heritage of community development could be harnessed for the survival of civic traditions under the central European conditions of the day. One of the motives was given by the institutional erosion driven by soviet-type rule: people were deprived in general of the effective chance for building and running their own institutions beyond the (repressed) private and family sphere. The apparatus of community development, accessible from a few foreign books in a Budapest library in the mid-1970s, looked both 'presentable' and suitable for resuscitating inhibited institutional functions, those of civil society included, at least within the compass of local communities.

The idea immediately met resistance, if not outright rejection, on two fronts: hardliners of the prevailing regime saw it as a Trojan assault on their externally imposed monopoly of power, while radicals of underground opposition circles regarded it, on the one hand, as too gradualist and, on the other hand, as amenable to manipulation by 'reformers' of a party-state that fundamentally was unreformable. The first paper in Hungarian to review the landscape of international community development was written and circulated in limited quarters with the support of the eminent reform politician Imre Pozsgay (then minister of culture, later one of the key figures in bringing down the

Berlin Wall and engineering the subsequent democratic transition in Hungary).

Eventually it was a small group of young professionals, most of whom graduated as 'adult educators', who actually followed up the tracks delineated in this paper. For quite some time they had been searching for ways to reinvigorate 'cultural policy' and 'community cultural centres' in the country. Discovering the mimeographed text, and an accompanying reader on community development methods, Tamás A. Varga, head of the group, concluded that the finding met several of the criteria they had in mind. The Hungarian Association for Community Development was founded by Varga and his wife, Ilona Vercseg, co-author of the present volume, in 1989, and celebrated the 20th anniversary of its establishment last year.

Civic concerns and development approaches may change and diverge considerably in the span of several decades across Europe, as is amply documented in the chapters that follow. But the accomplishment of the authors also attests to basic continuities and a common denominator in upholding, locally and day by day, the twin causes of freedom and community in our lands.

Attila Gergely
Budapest
11 January 2010

Acknowledgements

Many people have inspired and supported us in writing this book. It was through exchanges of ideas and experiences with members of the Combined European Bureau for Social Development that patterns and challenges of community development across Europe were initially explored. Only latterly have we come to realise and appreciate what a resource these exchanges are. We were also encouraged to pursue the idea of writing a book by friends and colleagues in our respective countries. Our thanks go to all of those involved, internationally and nationally.

It has been our families who have been closest to the planning and writing process. In Ilona's case, the involvement included a professional element: one of her sons, Tomi, translated her drafts from Hungarian to English and the other, Máté, provided material on training courses. Paul's wife Barbara encouraged him over many months and, in the final stages, his daughter Juliet and son Barney read and corrected chapters. Our heartfelt thanks to members of both families.

Edit Brull commented on Chapter Four, Graham Maney on Chapter Seven and Patience Seebohm on Chapter Eight. They gave their time and expertise generously. We were awarded a grant by the *Community Development Journal* to cover translation costs and we are grateful to the editorial board for recognising the need for this resource. We are very pleased that the journal's logo is included on the book's cover. We are also indebted to Emily Watt at The Policy Press for having guided us from the book's inception to its publication.

The ideas and examples in the publication have been informed by the willingness of many people – members of community groups, community development workers, policymakers and others – to share their rich experiences with us. We thank them deeply for this commitment

Acknowledgements

ONE

Introduction

As we planned this publication, we became increasingly aware of the significance for our work of major events – past and present – that have influenced the ideas and experiences that are discussed. The book was written 20 years after the fall of the Berlin Wall, the event that symbolised the collapse of communist regimes in Poland, Hungary, East Germany, Bulgaria, Romania and Czechoslovakia. In 1990, the changes reached Albania and Yugoslavia. Over the next three years, the Baltic nations, Ukraine and the countries of the southern Caucasus regained their independence. These events were as profound politically, economically and socially as they were sudden. Opportunities to re-examine the meaning and potential of 'community' became possible and the challenge of supporting social movements and related professions became increasingly evident. The concept of civil society was at the centre of debate and struggle, that of community development beginning to emerge.

The second context for the writing was the expanding membership of the European Union (EU), which brought with it a climate of continuing uncertainty over the political future of the continent. This has raised questions such as whether there will be increasing coherence between western European countries and those in central and eastern Europe or whether there will be fragmentation. Will the current dominance of the Right in European politics lead to clashes with progressive European traditions, with which advocates of civil society are mostly aligned, or will tolerance prevail? Finally, there is the issue of the hold on parts of the electorate of racist political parties and xenophobic attitudes: will support for them grow or weaken? These questions all point to hesitancy and doubts surrounding the idea of a united Europe.

The implications of the 2008–09 recession have become increasingly evident throughout Europe and the rest of the world. Its impact, however, has been uneven. Communities already experiencing disadvantages have seen a rise in unemployment and an increase in poverty. At the same time, the combination of mounting scientific evidence and campaigning by environmental groups has resulted in the issue of climate change becoming part of the mainstream political agenda of countries across the world. Politicians are beginning to face up to the policy implications of this. There is a realisation more generally that the use of energy resources, and therefore lifestyle, will have to change. Finally, in the UK context, the book is being published as a new government takes office. This follows a period of declining support for the previous Labour government and, as a result of the controversy over MPs' expenses, widespread disillusion with politicians.

Taken as a whole, these events and developments add up to more than merely the context or backdrop to our writing. They are of too great a magnitude for that. Each of them permeates every one of the themes and issues that we explore in the following chapters.

Origins

The starting points of the book provide a contrast to the canvas sketched out above. They are both modest and personal. The authors worked together from the early 1990s through the Combined European Bureau for Social Development (CEBSD). This is a small network of national community development organisations in Europe committed to sharing and developing community development practice and to informing and influencing European policies. Representatives meet regularly, visit projects, organise seminars and disseminate community development experiences and ideas. The main motivation for writing the book sprang from a wish to reflect on and draw out key learning that CEBSD examined and developed between 1992 and 2006, to share and clarify themes and to identify similarities and differences between community development in western Europe and community development in central and eastern Europe. As we shall explain, this was only possible by placing community development in the context of civil society, one of the themes at a key international conference held in Budapest in 2004 and organised by CEBSD, the Hungarian Association for Community Development (HACD) and the International Association for Community Development. Further experience of the connections between community development and civil society was gained by Ilona Vercseg through her international work within an East–East community development programme from 2000 to 2006 and through the Central and Eastern European Citizens Network from 2000 onwards.

The process of sharing ideas and analysis was strengthened as a result of bilateral visits and exchanges between Hungary and the UK. These focused mainly on rural community development, using a mix of training, seminars and visits. The experiences provided opportunities for the authors to deepen their understanding of community development in the two countries as well as to share their observations and ideas with colleagues. The close links forged between Hungary and the UK were designed to increase the skills and knowledge of the community development workers and local people who were involved in the visits. They also, however, provided an invaluable opportunity for the two authors to discuss their ideas. Increasingly, they found that these ran along very similar lines.

Central to the decision to write the book was the growing interest among a wide range of individuals and organisations wishing to understand the connections between civil society and community development. This was where the energy for planning and writing the book came from. It was, however, more than this. We were also increasingly aware of the importance of bringing a critical analysis to bear on the connections between civil society and community development. The reasons for taking this perspective can be broken down into the following components.

Analysis of the wider context

Seeking to understand underlying trends and influential ideas presents a major challenge for community groups and social movements. This is because any action that seeks to mobilise people has to stay close to their concerns. The action is played out at the micro level, focusing on the issues and arguments that are important to the participants. More often than not, the action and dialogue takes place at either the local community level or within identity and interest groups. Even social movements that operate globally have constantly to be aware of their constituencies – the commitments and beliefs of the people and groups who support them.

Being skilled at analysing the wider context is, however, of critical importance. Community development is especially vulnerable to the criticism that it can become wholly focused on local issues, the implication of the criticism being that local people are not encouraged to understand and act on issues in wider regional, national and international fora. Community development trainers will often urge participants to 'lift their heads from the grindstone', to take a step back from the demands of day-to-day practice and create space for reflection and exploration of how their work connects with wider agendas. This imperative was a major reason behind our decision to write this book, to explore community development and civil society through the experiences and learning of those involved but to do so within a broad analytical framework.

Reviewing community development

Both the position and nature of community development means that understanding and appraising it needs to be a continuous process. Community development takes place on the boundaries of different systems: communities, voluntary and statutory organisations, the political system and government; it is constantly moving between these and, by definition, it has to respond to changing circumstances. Inevitably, therefore, the community development profession has to be adept at handling changes happening around it – and be capable of changing itself. It can only do this if it is constantly asking questions of itself, engaging in debate and developing theory. A lively literature forms a key part of this attitude; the chapters that follow are a contribution to this. We seek to review ideas and theories and to either reaffirm or question them. This is done in the spirit of critical debate and with the intention of helping to improve community development's effectiveness.

The opportunity to compare the community development experiences of the UK and Hungary and, more broadly, western and central/eastern Europe, provides an additional dimension to the review process. From the early chapters, readers will be alert to the different contexts of community development in the UK and Hungary. However, we think they will also become aware of the commonalities of both values and practice in the two countries. The origins and the structures of community development reflect the societies of which they are a part. There are nuanced differences between the practice. Yet the fundamental architecture of community development is the same.

Understanding civil society

Historians and commentators will continue to debate for a long time the extent to which the changes in central and eastern Europe that began in 1989 heralded a new kind of political movement. At the heart of the new political order has been the concept of civil society: the idea that there can be associations and social movements that complement, as well as challenge, the dominant political system. It is a concept of fundamental importance in central and eastern Europe, as it is in many other parts of the globe. There are, however, differences between the term's meaning in central and eastern Europe and how it is used in the western European context. It was our growing awareness of these differences that motivated us to have civil society as a central pillar in our analysis.

Our interest turns primarily on the following questions. Is the idea of civil society essentially the preserve of the intelligentsia or does it reach out to other groups in society? What does the map of involvement in civil society look like? It is the potential scope for extending and deepening the concept of civil society that concerns us.

Bringing together community development and civil society

The book accordingly examines the connections between community development and civil society. More specifically, it aims to set out the contribution that community development can make to strengthening civil society. It draws on the authors' experiences and knowledge of community development and civil society. More importantly, it is a means by which the voices of those most involved in social change activities at the community level can be heard. We use their stories and case studies of practice both to point to their achievements and to identify challenges and weaknesses facing social movements and the community development profession.

Readership

The reasons outlined above for preparing the publication might suggest that it has been written exclusively for members of social movements/community groups and community development workers. This is far from being the case. Community development interventions and actions taken by civil society organisations connect with other key audiences at several levels:

• To maximise community development's potential, involving other players or stakeholders is essential. In the UK context, the power of the middle manager either to support or block the work of front-line staff such as community development workers is well known. It is therefore vital that individuals holding such positions have a good understanding of community development principles and practice. We are also aware of the potential for other professionals, such as youth workers, planning officers and education workers, to draw on community development knowledge and skills in their work. The book's content is as relevant to them as it is to middle managers. We hope, too, that it will inform the thinking and planning of policymakers – senior politicians, civil servants and local authority officers – whose decisions about resources and services are of critical importance for communities.

- The publication has a European focus. However, the ideas and actions explored connect with experiences and developments in other regions of the world. Hopefully, they can inform discussions and joint work undertaken through international networks and non-governmental organisations (NGOs). Ensuring that Europe remains open to community development and civil society ideas and principles from elsewhere in the world is essential, particularly from countries where there are rich community development traditions, for example, North America, Australia, New Zealand, Hong Kong, India, South Africa and many southern countries.
- New communities are forming all the time. In the UK, for example, since 2004 the number of migrant workers from the accession countries to the EU has increased significantly. There has also been an increase in the number of refugees and asylum seekers. The ideas and practices of community development and civil society will be relevant to all three of these communities. If they have not done so already, new communities will seek to make use of community development and civil society and they will want to draw from the experiences of other communities and social movements.
- There will also be new community leaders and community development workers. We argue later that a growing number of the latter are likely to join the profession as a result of their involvement in community groups rather than from the more traditional routes offered by higher education institutions. Again, this new 'generation' will want to learn about the emergence of community development and civil society ideas.

The publication aims to be of use to the above range of interests and actors in addition to addressing the concerns of community development and civil society groups, organisations and professions.

Finally, readers will become aware that the authors take a definite generalist approach to their topic. The subject matter discussed covers a range of disciplines and issues on the assumption that the principles behind community development and civil society offer a framework and that they can be applied to a surprising number of issues ranging from rural development and planning to social work and community education. This stance stands in contrast to global trends that recognise and encourage specialisation within disciplines, usually backed up by requirements for qualifications. It would be wrong, however, to infer that the generalist nature of community development and civil society as we define them can be equated with a low level of skills and a rudimentary knowledge base. On the contrary, it is precisely the extent of the demands made of community development and civil society that underlines the need for them to be clear as to what they stand for and what they can offer.

Structure

The fusion of key concepts with specific issues is reflected in the book's structure. The chapters in the middle section (Chapters Four to Eight) make use of a typology (explained in Chapter Two) put forward some years ago by an American sociologist. These are flanked by more generalist chapters that discuss themes and learning that are anticipated and identified in the more specialised chapters. This structure will become clearer through the following summary of the content of each of the chapters.

Chapter Two sets out the essential elements of the concept of civil society. It acknowledges the extent to which it is a contested concept. It also emphasises the distinctiveness of the concept for many people and organisations in central and eastern Europe. The authors explain their preference for an associational definition of civil society. They tackle the long-standing problem of giving meaning to the concept of community and then set out their rationale for choosing to use the typology of the sociologist Roland Warren. The typology proposes five key functions needed by communities to survive and flourish. This section of the chapter provides the book's framework. It ends by putting forward a hypothesis as to how community development can help communities be part of civil society.

Chapter Three provides a baseline definition and understanding of community development. It discusses its social movement and professional elements and then summarises its emergence in different regions of the world. It gives greater detail on community development's origins in the UK and Hungary. This chapter's broad scan reinforces both the internationalism of community development and its rich diversity.

Chapter Four is where the book moves into providing more specific material. It engages with the first of Warren's five functions required for a community really to exist – socialisation. Warren uses this concept to draw attention to the fundamental importance of community for individuals in the societal context. The chapter discusses the significance of community-based learning in community development and gives examples from Hungary, Denmark and Germany. It then discusses active citizenship, community schools and eco-schools. It concludes by linking these themes to democracy, again giving supporting examples.

Chapter Five analyses Warren's second function required for a community to be effective – economic wealth. It begins by separating out different strands or types of community economic development. It then examines the situation in central and eastern Europe, providing three case studies, before discussing the connections between community economic development and community development. This leads to an examination of two community economic development approaches that have widespread support in the UK – social entrepreneurship and asset-based community development. The chapter ends by summarising underlying theories of community economic development.

Chapter Six addresses the issue of social participation, first, the reasons why people are or are not prepared to become involved with community issues and, second, the potential dangers surrounding participation. It can be misused as well as used. The chapter then links the issue of participation to the theory of social capital, with the latter being analysed in the Hungarian context. The chapter concludes by referring to the concept of social inclusion and the participatory assumptions that are implicit in it.

Chapter Seven focuses on social control. It seeks to identify and specify how community development may be able to make a more substantive contribution to this issue than it does at present. Warren's typology is clear that social control requires community members to observe certain values and it is this that provides the basis for the chapter's argument. The chapter examines the connections between punishment and community and then opens up a broader framework for enabling communities to be more involved in social control. At the end of the chapter, a Hungarian community development perspective on social control is presented.

Chapter Eight explores the last of Warren's five functions. He refers to mutual support and solidarity. In the western European context, the term 'community care' is more likely to be used. The chapter begins by setting the scene for connecting community care and community development. Two case studies are then presented, one in the UK and one in Hungary. This material provides the context for the setting out of seven principles that can be used to guide a community development approach to community care. The chapter concludes by emphasising the importance of this approach, both for individuals in communities and for social policy.

Chapter Nine takes up the question of how well equipped community development is to respond both to the challenges set out in the preceding five chapters and to changes taking place globally. The connections between community development and civil society are reaffirmed. The chapter specifies particular challenges facing community development in Hungary and the UK and ends by pointing to those that are shared by the two countries and those that are different.

Chapter Ten examines the extent to which community development can turn to systems of learning and support. Information is provided on current and planned learning opportunities in Hungary. This is followed by an analysis of the current training situation in the UK, with particular reference to England. In a brief final section, a European perspective on learning and support is given. Again, the authors use the contrasting contexts across Europe to point to common themes and challenges.

Chapter Eleven draws together the authors' ideas, focusing on the question of how the contribution of community development to strengthening civil society can be specified. They return to the five ways in which community development might strengthen civil society suggested in Chapter Two, submitting them to critical comment in the light of the content of the intervening chapters. They then identify three key areas of challenge – the community development profession, communities and civil society – before setting out possible future scenarios for community development. In a concluding section, they first re-state the need for community development to continue to struggle to hold the balance between providing support for grassroots action and engagement with policy issues; second, they highlight the paramount importance of three agenda items facing community development and civil society: reaffirmation of the need to strengthen participatory democracy, responding to the continuing existence of poverty and social exclusion, and challenging racism and xenophobia.

The authors have written the book collaboratively in the sense that they have both contributed to all the chapters. Readers will sometimes be aware of the different assumptions of each author, as well as their different writing styles. We have not ironed out these features as they give a signal of the different contexts from which the authors come.

We have sought to give the book a clear structure, enabling points and themes to be developed. Most of the chapters, however, are self-standing and can be read and used as such.

TWO

Civil society

Introduction

Civil society, like the concepts of democracy, liberalism and radicalism, is a 'catch-all' term. It is a phrase that has profound relevance to societies across the globe and that is part of the mainstream of political theory, social policy and the agendas of social movements. It has become a melting pot into which ideas, arguments and examples are poured ceaselessly. Yet this topicality is in danger of rendering the term meaningless.

There can be no doubt as to the complexity surrounding the concept, particularly given that it is used in so many different political, economic and social contexts. It requires us to engage with the fundamental building blocks of society: democracy, human rights, participation, social justice and communities. Hence we should not be surprised to find that it is a concept that has been, and continues to be, strongly debated.

In the context of the UK, the term civil society is used broadly to refer to two phenomena: evidence and anxiety about some of the weaknesses of the representative political system and recognition of the growing significance of associational life. Out of the first of these has emerged the language of new citizenship. This is the approach taken by the Power Inquiry (2006), which gives the findings of a wide-ranging investigation into Britain's democracy. In a chapter entitled 'The rise of new citizens', the inquiry's report draws attention to the vibrancy and innovation of forms of participation that contrast with the disengagement and alienation from formal democracy. Concerns about the health of traditional political processes, as well as clear evidence of disillusioned voters, have spawned a considerable literature and intense scrutiny of the topic by think tanks such as Demos and the Institute for Public Policy Research. Commenting on the European Parliament elections of June 2009, the European Policy Centre noted that the overall turnout of approximately 43 per cent of the 375 million eligible voters in Europe represented an historical low and displayed 'the high degree of apathy and lack of interest already apparent throughout the electoral campaign across the 27 member states' (www.epc.eu).

There can be little doubt that the issue of citizenship in contemporary politics is recognised as a priority by senior politicians, academics, think tanks and citizen organisations. It is lodged clearly as a serious concern. Responses and action, however, are in shorter supply. The crisis at Westminster in 2009 over MPs' expenses claims re-enforced public disillusion with the representational system; at the time of writing, this had cast a shadow over the run-up to the 2010 general election.

Our second phenomenon is scrutinised and debated with equal zeal. The Carnegie UK Trust's Commission on Civil Society describes associational life as 'the space' of organised activity undertaken neither by the government nor by for-private-profit business (Daly with Howell, 2006, p 6). This means that a wide-ranging list of formal and informal associations is included, from a variety of non-governmental organisations (NGOs) and trade unions to political parties, professional associations, faith groups and social movements. We shall argue that it is community groups and social movements that lie at the heart of the associational dimension of civil society. Our starting point is with the following questions: what does civil society mean for ordinary people? To what extent can citizens become involved in civil society? How can they be supported to do so?

The systemic transition that began in many parts of central and eastern Europe at the end of the 1980s were linked with a much more urgent and dynamic understanding of civil society that rediscovered notions of collective social consciousness:

> Self-mobilisation from below, in different grassroots activities, gradually emerged. With increasing recognition of the escalating political and economic crises, the silenced citizen was step-by-step replaced with more open dialogue among formerly isolated circles of independently-minded citizens. Cautiously, the media became involved in the new critical discourse. The long list of taboo themes began to shrink. In other words, a new public arena emerged to openly and critically discuss social, environmental, cultural and, in a restricted way, political issues. (Jensen and Miszlivetz, 2003, p 20)

If we take the example of Hungary, the pulling down of the one-party, dictatorial and centralised structures has had to be accompanied by a commitment to support the emergence of multi-party, democratic and decentralised structures:

The path to interpreting the meaning of civil society leads through naming democracy and citizenship. Comprehending the essence of democracy became increasingly complex during the ten years since the change of regime. Our recent experiences also prove that the main issue is around the acquirement and maintenance of power. (Vercseg, 1999, p 4)

Civil society organisations have existed in Hungarian public life for many years and yet the representatives of governmental organisations remain much more active than those involved in civil society organisations. There is a long way to go before the role of the state and its institutions will be sufficiently counter-balanced.

In general, civil society in central and eastern Europe is less focused on associational life than in western Europe. Groups tend to be more formally organised in central and eastern European countries. Informal forms of organisation, including social movements, are often not considered to be part of the spectrum of associations. Furthermore, the concept of civil society is extended to include the attitudes and behaviour of people. Miszlivetz argues that the main characteristics of civil society are to be found in the public domain, with reflexivity as its essence:

Civil society is ... a public zone, a sphere of solidarity where various interests are articulated and confront each other, where conflicts take place between individuals, groups and organisations.... Civil society relates to all of these, it is a kind of reflexivity, not a collection of organisations. It is the natural interaction that is important, that is what generates a force field in which civil society comes into being. (Miszlivetz, 1999, p 427)

The term 'reflexivity' refers to the processes of questioning, examining and becoming aware of the personal and professional and is closely connected to the concept of critical community practice (Butcher et al, 2007). It is distinguishable from the term 'reflection', which tends to be associated with practitioners examining what happened or is happening in a piece of practice.

If we accept that civil society contains reflexivity's scope for action, it is clear, paradoxically, that non-action, the lack of organisation, indifference and alienation are all types of a lack of reflexivity. Community development in Hungary and other countries in the region is concerned primarily with changing these kinds of reflexivity. It is people who form civil society, regardless of whether or not they are involved in the institutional and interactive processes of society.

By referring to the different contexts of the UK and Hungary, we are highlighting the need to avoid the fallacy of suggesting that there is one, uniform meaning of civil society. Differences of experience and definition are to be found as much within western Europe and central and eastern Europe as between them. This point is emphasised by Gerard Hautekeur when discussing the context of a survey of community development organisations:

> The national Social Cultural Planning Office in the Netherlands, in its annual report for the year 2000, makes a comparison among a number of European countries. It demonstrates that the Netherlands and the Scandinavian countries are characterised by a high level of organisation in civil society. At the other extreme of the spectrum we find France and other southern European countries with a low level of organisation. The remaining countries of western Europe are somewhere in the middle. (Hautekeur, 2005, p 389)

Our concern in this volume is to explore the theories, traditions and practice of civil society across Europe. There are also, of course, powerful traditions and practice across many southern countries, the US and elsewhere that we do not address. We hold that at the core of the concept of civil society there are shared values and principles, albeit the application of the concept, how it is used, is very different. Thus we are alerting the reader to the framework within which this book has been conceived: not only the connections between civil society and community development, but also the different experiences and meanings of civil society.

In this chapter we begin by examining the concept of civil society in more depth. This analysis will convey the authors' approach to understanding and defining civil society and its direct relevance to community development. We will then connect this discussion to the concept of community, introducing the five functions of community that are examined in more depth in Chapters Four to Eight. We end the chapter with an outline of how community development can act as a bridge between communities and civil society, thereby setting the scene for subsequent chapters. Our aim is to provide answers to the question: why put civil society and community development together?

Both are about hope and change and both are rooted in people's experiences, but how do the two concepts interrelate?

Definitions and disagreements

When social scientists and others refer to concepts that are contested they wish to convey more than disagreements about meaning and definition – important though these are. They are pointing also to disagreements that are political and ideological. This is certainly the case with the term 'civil society'. Some Marxists, for example, argue that civil society simply reproduces social relations and conflicts of interest characteristic of advanced capitalist societies. Others question the eagerness with which institutions and governments have embraced the language of civil society. Hakan Seckinelgin, for example, analyses civil society as a metaphor for western liberalism, using institutions like the World Bank and the UK's Department for International Development to discuss the argument (Seckinelgin, 2002).

That civil society is far from being a neutral concept has become increasingly evident, as its language has gone beyond its European origins to reach almost every country in the world. Keane underlines the significance of this:

> Tomorrow's historians may well conclude that the spreading talk of civil society was not just talk. They may highlight the fact that something new was born in the world – the unprecedented (if unevenly distributed) growth of the sense within NGOs and publics at large that civilians live in one world, and that they have obligations to other civilians living beyond their borders, simply because they are civilians. (Keane, 2003, p 36)

One recognised way of understanding civil society is to locate it as one of three sectors, alongside the state and the market. There are, however, debates as to how it connects with the state and about its relationship to market forces. In these debates the potential for confusing empirical and normative definitions of civil society is considerable: how civil society actually is and a vision of how or what it should be. The distinction by Michael Edwards between three main schools of thought on civil society is helpful:

> Civil society as a *part* of society (the neo-Toquevillian school that focuses on associational life), civil society as a *kind* of

society (characterised by positive norms and values as well as
success in meeting particular social goals), and civil society
as the *public sphere*. (Edwards, 2004, p 10)

In a report for the Carnegie UK Trust, Siobhan Daly and Jude Howell
use this distinction and provide a useful summary of the debates about
how civil society relates to the state and to market forces (Daly with
Howell, 2006, pp 14–15). Our approach to the question 'What is civil
society?' has been indicated already. We align ourselves with those who
see the vital importance for any society to have space between the
state and the public within which community groups, campaigning
organisations and social movements can be active. This understanding
of civil society is necessary for any democracy. Inevitably, there are
areas and examples between the state, civil society and the market that
overlap and that are unclear – social enterprises and credit unions, for
example, exist on the boundary between civil society and the market.

The relationships between civil society, the state and the market are
dynamic: they are subject to change over time and in varying contexts.
This is a key theme that emerges from the contributions to the volume
edited by Purdue (2007). While we maintain that civil society needs to
keep hold of the distinct space between government and the market,
we think that it is essential, conceptually, for there to be connections
between all three parts of the framework – the state, the market and
associations – and, in the cut and thrust of the real world, there needs
to be communication and collaboration between them. Indeed, it can
be argued that, in a world increasingly dominated by global corporate
interests, it will become more important for governments to work
closely with civil society organisations in order to constrain commercial
and financial forces. The definition of civil society used by the London
School of Economics' Centre for Civil Society makes the point well. It
begins by referring to civil society as 'the arena of uncoerced collective
action around shared interests, purposes and values' but goes on to state
that 'in practice, the boundaries between state, civil society, family and
market are often complex, blurred and negotiated' (www.lse.ac.uk/
collections/CCS).

The idea of civil society as a link between the state and the public
is captured by Ernest Gellner, a strong supporter of the thinking and
action that took place in central and eastern Europe at the end of the
1980s. Civil society is:

That set of non-governmental institutions which is
strong enough to counterbalance the state and, while

not preventing the state from fulfilling its role of keeper of the peace and arbitrator amongst major interests, can nevertheless prevent it from dominating and atomising the rest of society. (Gellner, 1994, p 5)

We are aware that, in positioning ourselves within the associational domain of civil society, we lay ourselves open to the criticism that we are falling into the trap of articulating both a narrow and a romanticised approach: narrow because we are giving low priority to civil society as a public good and as consisting of a wide range of organisations, and romantic because we are assuming that civil society always manifests itself in positive forms. We are happy to acknowledge the first of these criticisms; our commitment is to understanding informal, often untidy and vulnerable organisations, groups and networks. It is these that, from our perspective, give civil society such deep significance. We refute, however, the second criticism. Indeed, we are alert to two potentially negative features of associational civil society. The first of these is referred to by Keane (1998) as 'uncivil' society, the incivility, intolerance and violence that can be observed in many societies. Indeed, he argues that there is an inner contradiction within civil society – every civil society tends to produce a violent antithesis. In the context of central and eastern Europe, the discrimination faced by many Roma communities illustrates the negative aspect of civil society, particularly as the situation of these communities worsened after the collapse of communism:

> Since most countries in central and eastern Europe are not capable of protecting Roma rights and ensuring their safety, many Roma feel increasingly threatened and insecure. Such experiences have made them suspicious and wary of the outside world. (Schuringa, 2005, p 15)

Given that civil society is essential for democracy, the need for individuals and organisations to be vigilant about its principles and practice, and how it can go badly wrong, is of paramount importance. It should not be forgotten that, in extreme circumstances, civil society can deteriorate all too rapidly into civil war. The relationship between civil society and community development can gain a special importance when there is conflict. One of the key instruments for promoting social integration is communication; formulating one's situation and defining the problem can lead to the emergence of genuine dialogue and this, in turn, can lead to mutual understanding and accord. Community development helps to break through communication barriers and achieve active participation – the road to solidarity comes from communicative action and cooperation.

The second potentially negative feature of associational civil society is sometimes played out at the micro, community level. Community development seeks to mobilise and organise people around issues and needs, the resolution of which will lead to stronger communities. It taps into the positive, aspirational motivations of people, often working off a combination of people's self-interest and their altruism; being part of a housing campaign, for example, can lead to a higher quality local environment that will benefit both the individuals directly involved and the community as a whole. However, the assumption that people will think and act positively does not always hold up. People who become involved can be intolerant towards other members of their community or cynical and dismissive of the efforts made by other groups and organisations. It is mistaken to think that if the people involved in a protest against authority are oppressed, the focus of that protest must necessarily be progressive. That is not necessarily the case. Oppressed people can just as easily turn their anger and frustration against the wrong targets, rather than against those that are the cause of their oppression. This was apparent in Bradford, Burnley and Oldham, towns in northern England where, in 2001, there were serious clashes between Asian and white people. White working-class residents who themselves have experienced oppression are as likely to turn against those who are also oppressed but whom they – often falsely – judge to be less oppressed.

Civil society and community

If our focus is on groups, organisations and networks that provide a crucially important community base for civil society, how do we pin down the elusive concept of community? This question continues to challenge philosophers, sociologists and many others, including advocates of community development and community-based programmes. It is a source of frustration and disagreement, especially among those who feel that attempts to specify its meaning are too backward-looking. These attempts assume, it is argued, a too optimistic and romantic interpretation of community as close-knit, harmonious neighbourhoods (Bauman, 2001). Recognition of the growing significance of identity communities of, for example, faith, race and gender has done something to counter this assumption. However, attempts at providing definitions still, it is contended, fail to take account of fundamental changes in society brought about by the increased dominance of individualism and the inward-looking, protective nature of growing numbers of communities – 'gated' communities, for example, which place affluent individuals and families in a cocoon, surrounded by walls and patrolled by security guards. Finally, critics argue that too many definitions of community ignore or underestimate the impact of the internet and other technological changes. 'Virtual' communities are now part of contemporary language and behaviour and the use of social networking groups, email groups, 'blogging' and chat rooms has expanded significantly in recent years.

Perhaps the concept of civil society can lead us to a more modern interpretation of community because it synthesises two seemingly contradictory yet very basic human needs: belonging and freedom. At the centre of civil society are not organisations but the citizen, who, according to Dahrendorf:

> needs both attachment and the possibility of choice to fully achieve his [sic] life possibilities. And this attachment requires variations of autonomous coalitions which we call civil society. (Dahrendorf, 1997, p 48)

This approach is significant because it incorporates the importance of the security a community can provide through attachments as well as individual freedom through choices; the unity, in other words, of community and civil society. If either one is missing or weak, the need to use community development principles, methods, knowledge and skills to intervene and to bring about change becomes very apparent.

We need constantly to update ourselves when seeking to understand communities, their diversity and complexity and how they are addressing, or coping with, change. We also need to remind ourselves of the extensive and long-standing theoretical literature on community. According to the great theorists of German community theory (Herder, Schiller, Hegel, Tonnies), community is an organic formation in which the whole person is incorporated. Society, on the other hand, is inorganic and functional, incorporating the individual only in fragmented ways (mainly as a result of the division of labour). Juxtaposing community and functionality raises key questions for community theory. It is outside the scope of this volume to engage with these in any detail. It is important, however, to explain why we have chosen a functional community theory to support the idea that the concepts of community development and civil society are symbiotic and that it is this unity that informs, in a profound sense, community development practice.

We have turned to the work of a sociologist, writing nearly 50 years ago (the first edition of *The community in America* was published in 1963), to provide the framework for Chapters Four to Eight. Roland Warren argued that, for a community really to exist, it has to fulfil the following five functions:

- socialisation, through which the community implants certain values into its members;
- economic wealth, through which the community ensures the livelihoods of its members;
- social participation – fulfilling the general need for socialisation;
- social control, which demands that members should observe certain community values;
- mutual support, a process through which community members carry out tasks that are too big or too urgent to be handled by an individual alone.

These five functions, according to Warren, prevail formally or informally in a multitude of forms from rural settlements to major cities. Whatever the local characteristics, the functions are always present in all human groups that sociologists call communities. Warren states that, while all the functions are relevant to localities, they are not necessarily functions over which the community exercises exclusive responsibility or over which it has total control:

> On the contrary, the organisation of society to perform these functions at the community level involves a strong tie between locally based units such as businesses, schools, governments and voluntary associations, and social systems extending far beyond the confines of the community. (Warren, 1963, p 10)

This caveat is of crucial importance for community development because, while it always engages with people in their localities and networks, its remit and objectives are much broader. The last thing that community development wants to do is to imply that somehow people and their ideas and ambitions are trapped within their neighbourhoods or networks.

Why have we chosen to use Warren's five functions? What are their relevance to civil society and community in the 21st century? Why are they useful as a framework for a publication on civil society and community development? The following are the advantages:

- The five functions provide a welcome element of *clarity* for the application of a complex concept. Each stated function is self-explanatory and, when taken together, the functions set out a clear framework.
- The functions span a welcome *breadth* of activity, from social interaction (individually and collectively), to economic development, participation and consultation, social control within and by communities and, finally, informal mutual support and community involvement.
- There is a *universal* quality to the functions. They apply internationally to a variety of cultural and social contexts. This is important because of the tendency for understanding community to be weighed down by the Anglo-Saxon empirical tradition of the study of community – detailed case studies of villages and small towns.
- The functions offer the opportunity to discuss communities in very *human* terms. The functions are people-oriented. This too is important because of our wish to examine local community development within the context of global civil society. We move between the two in the chapters that follow and it is essential that we avoid drifting into abstractions, thereby losing the essential human essence of community development and civil society.
- The functions are not set in stone. On the contrary, they are *adaptable*. Two critical principles follow from this. First, we can acknowledge the differences both within and between communities. This is of paramount importance when exploring the links between civil society and community development. Second, we avoid the trap of equating community only with locality. While it was designed originally with this focus in mind, the framework can also be used to understand communities of common interest, of shared identity and communities that consist of informal networks. All three of these are central to contemporary definitions of community development because of the ways in which communities cohere and organise themselves:

> Many people feel they belong to several communities simultaneously. Their networks are flexible and strategic, depending on the social and political context, as well as their personal circumstances and choices. (Gilchrist, 2004, p 4)

The extent to which the fivefold framework demonstrates these advantages will be tested in Chapters Four to Eight. While the thrust of each of these chapters is to explain and illustrate the connections between civil society and community development, the arena in which these take place is community. Communities exist as much more than merely the context or material for civil society and community development. They are the lifeblood for both. Without an understanding of community, civil society and community development risk being empty vessels, arid terms that lack substance. This should be the riposte to sceptics who question the possibility of giving meaning to the term 'community'. We should remember also that it is a term with which a number of disciplines and interventions have to struggle. Anthony Giddens makes this point in relation to politics:

> The theme of community is fundamental to the new politics, but not just as an abstract slogan. The advance of globalisation makes a community focus both necessary and possible, because of the downward pressure it exerts. 'Community' doesn't imply trying to recapture lost forms of local solidarity; it refers to practical means of furthering the social and material refurbishment of neighbourhoods, towns and larger local areas. (Giddens, 1998, p 79)

It is the awareness of the community imperative that explains the interest globally in the phenomenon of social capital (Putnam, 2000). This places the issue of trust and cooperation firmly on the public agenda. When a government is faced with the challenge of divided communities and of neighbourhoods virtually destroyed by violence, threatening behaviour and high levels of crime and drug abuse, finding ways of re-injecting social capital becomes a vitally important goal. Thus community becomes an essential part of the policy agenda as well as being at the core of civil society and community development.

Our contention is that the idea of civil society connects with the essence of community development – the latter's transformational capacity, its potential for opening up pathways to learning and its commitment to collective action as an essential and integral part of democratic practice. Community development can help create an organised civil society in the community. Therefore the question of organisation and non-organisation is again put in the limelight, particularly in the new European democracies where civil society faces difficulties in organising itself. Community intervention can speed up the processes that are potentially present in communities but that require a great deal of encouragement and different forms of empowerment to become manifest in organised ways.

The need to be listened to can develop into civil action if citizens discuss and adjust their points of view, establishing a collective position that can be represented effectively in decision-making arenas. Only an organised framework can provide meaningful opportunities to define who we are and what our objectives are, and to make plans and implement them. Being organised is a precondition for being able to respond effectively to opportunities. More broadly, the development of civil society's organisations stands for the growth of participative democracy, meaning an increased level of participation in public affairs from preparing and making decisions to implementing them.

Connecting community development and civil society

We conclude this chapter by outlining and illustrating five ways in which community development can help communities to be part of civil society: challenging, defending, maintaining, recognising and strengthening civil society. This will set the scene and provide an introduction to the myriad of ways in which the two concepts connect in the community and practice contexts.

Challenging civil society

There is a cutting edge to community development that can result in community groups posing tough questions to power-holders and to organisations such as local authorities that are responsible for delivering services. The local knowledge of community groups, local support and the likelihood that members will be highly motivated means that often they will have a strong voice. Within a broad definition of civil society, one that includes trade unions, faith groups and voluntary/community organisations, this watchdog role is one that is particularly suited to community groups.

Challenging civil society can be undertaken in a confrontational way, each side, as it were, lined up against each other. This tends to be the style adopted by the Community Organising movement that originated in the campaigns led and inspired by Saul Alinsky in the US and that more recently has been active in the UK. Strongly committed to campaigning for social justice, the movement is particularly active in London. Called London Citizens, the campaign is, for example, seeking to ensure that poor people benefit from public funding being invested for the 2012

Olympic Games. The main tactic is confrontational. Power-holders are challenged very directly, based on careful calculations of what can be gained from any situation. Community Organising concentrates on a single issue at any one time.

  Confrontation tactics, however, are not the only way for community development to challenge civil society. Targeted lobbying or being active members of partnership boards can be equally effective. So, too, can forming coalitions with campaigning organisations that are likely to have wider contacts and breadth of experience than community groups. The latter, however, can bring a strong grassroots perspective to an issue. The following example of campaigning against an extremist political party illustrates how community development can provide a key strand of the work.

Hope Not Hate

Hope Not Hate Yorkshire was set up in 2006 to campaign against the British National Party (BNP) and to strengthen communities to resist racism. It undertakes political campaigning, working with political parties and elected members to tackle the BNP. It also works closely with trade unions, seeking to ensure that anti-fascist activity across the region is put on the agendas of trade unions.

Hope Not Hate also works with communities at a local level. An example is when two community centres in a predominantly white, deprived council estate in the town of Keighley were asked to host surgeries for the local BNP councillor. Their immediate instinct was to refuse. They were unsure, however, how to do this. Hope Not Hate worked closely with the groups concerned, looking at their constitutions and equal opportunities policies to ensure these were robust. This work enabled the groups to reject the BNP on the basis that they are a racist party. Hope Not Hate had advised the centres how they could use democratic means to reject the BNP.

This type of work builds naturally. One group of people challenging the BNP or racism gives others the courage to stand up and be counted. The positive stories of this are collated and used in anti-fascist leaflets, further raising community awareness as well as supporting the political aims of Hope Not Hate. Stories and ideas are further shared through contacts and work undertaken on a local, regional and national level.

This example demonstrates that community development has an important part to play in challenging civil society. It can inject a particular dimension into the democratic process.

Defending civil society

Sometimes the right of people to act freely, without interference, needs to be supported. This is where community development has a role to play in defending civil society. A small example: a community group in Liverpool was scheduled to have a meeting to prepare a funding application to the local regeneration agency. The community development worker who was supporting the group had heard on the grapevine that an evangelical organisation intent on expanding its work in the city planned to send representatives to the meeting. At the opening of the meeting, the worker turned to the representatives and explained that the meeting was only for the group. She asked the representatives to leave, which, somewhat surprised, they did. This was an example of community development defending the right of a key component of civil society to exist independently and freely. A more complex example follows:

> ### Participation and the Practice of Rights Project
>
> The Participation and the Practice of Rights Project (PPR) is a coalition of groups and organisations in Ireland with a focus on north Dublin and north Belfast. It aims to demonstrate how a 'rights-based approach' can be used within deprived communities. A feasibility study in 2004 indicated that people at the local level are often unable to access rights and services because they have been denied access to participation in decision making.
>
> The project then began to test out a model of how to build capacity and knowledge within communities so that access to rights and services could be monitored. The project uses the model to challenge and change policy and processes. Issues on which the project has worked include support for families who have been bereaved through suicide and who are campaigning for improved mental health services in north Belfast, and drug users campaigning for the allocation of medical cards in north Dublin.
>
> Members of the coalition believe that fundamental change is required in how governance is delivered. The project provides an opportunity to develop a model to change the nature of participation in governance and, in doing so, bring about access to justice, rights and the delivery of services for those most in need (www.pprproject.org).

PPR is an example of how community development can contribute to the defence of civil society. It gathered evidence of the extent to which groups of people were being denied opportunities, thereby weakening or undermining civil society. It is now seeking to change this situation.

Maintaining civil society

Sometimes community development should take an active part in helping to ensure the continuation of civil society. This is when community development's role is to help maintain civil society. Here, community development will tend to be involved organisationally. In the UK context this role has often been required when partnership boards have been set up in regeneration areas. In such situations it is essential for there to be representation on boards from a diverse range of communities and community groups. For only large community groups or voluntary organisations to be represented is to condone too narrow a definition of civil society. We know that there is an active sector of small community groups and networks and, for the sake of the health of civil society, it is essential that they are represented. The term 'voluntary and community sector' is used throughout the UK to re-enforce this point. Nevertheless, there have been many examples in recent years of the tensions that can surround community group representation on partnership boards set up by government programmes:

> If regeneration partnerships are to be empowering rather than disempowering for the most marginalised individuals and groups, there needs to be continuing support. This includes the need for community development facilitation and infrastructure support as well as the need for training – to meet the learning needs of communities as they themselves define these. (Mayo and Taylor, 2001, p 50)

Community development can also help to maintain civil society by supporting service delivery – not being part of the delivery process itself but preparing the ground for it. This can be observed in community care work that relies on the mobilisation of volunteers and members of community groups to support vulnerable people in the community, particularly people with mental health difficulties, elderly and disabled people. Community development can play a key role in sustaining those parts of civil society that do not receive help from state or voluntary services. It connects with the tradition of self-help and mutual support. We expand this idea in Chapter Eight.

Recognising civil society

Community development is only one of a number of approaches and interventions in civil society. It can only be a partial response to social, economic and environmental problems that afflict communities. It is important, therefore, for community development to point to other organisations that are essential for a thriving civil society, notably trade unions, voluntary organisations, faith groups, campaigning organisations and international social movements. This is how community development can contribute to ensuring the recognition of civil society. It is an advocacy role, giving support to partner organisations and adding its voice to arguments made to governments and international agencies to avoid interfering with the independence and freedom required for civil society. Examples can be found locally, regionally and nationally as well as at the European level.

Strengthening civil society

In one sense, all of the four roles outlined above are geared towards the strengthening of civil society. They all aim to ensure the continuation, vitality and independence of civil society. There is, however, a different and equally important meaning attached to the notion of strengthening civil society that lies within the realm of the imagination: how a 'better' society can be envisaged, what changes are needed to bring this about and how these can be resourced.

The capacity to imagine a different future is at the heart of community development. Sometimes it can appear to be over-idealistic or naïve, but a belief in the possibility of change and improvement is implicit within community development thinking. Community development can also respond to the constant need for the renewal of communities, especially in the context of shifting cultures. At a general level, community development is essentially an optimistic stance about human nature and creativity. More particularly, it is saying that civil society has a key role to play both now and in the future and that it needs to be thought about, debated, planned and resourced.

Ways in which community development can challenge, defend, maintain, recognise and strengthen civil society will be drawn out in the chapters that follow. There is an inter-dependence between community development and civil society that can make it hard to distinguish between them. The process of identifying the distinctive qualities of community development that connect it with civil society will be ongoing. At this point we have only made a start on the journey.

THREE

Community development

Community development has always been vulnerable to criticism that it is a term that is both vague and pretentious – claiming too much. Let us begin by taking two examples of how community development tackles local issues:

- A community association based in an urban neighbourhood negotiates with the local authority to have a local refuse tip closed because of evidence of leaking gases. The tip is filled in, grassed over and becomes a small environmental park. It is owned by the local authority but is maintained and serviced through a partnership agreement between the community association and the local authority.
- In a former coal mining area, a development trust is set up to tackle issues of unemployment and lack of investment. Achievements include the development of a former café as the base for a wide range of local services including space let to tenants and £1.3 million investment in new office premises to meet demand for rented space and provide new community facilities.

In the first example, we can see traces of the tradition of self-help as well as the contemporary emphasis on partnership working, both themes associated closely with the northern European experience of community development. The project is making a modest contribution to the community. In the second example, there is evidence of community development being strongly linked with the local economy and it is seeking to make a significant impact on economic and social development. It is ambitious.

Part of the problem when discussing community development is uncertainty about its scope. On what scale is it operating? Is it essentially about voluntary involvement or does it depend on there being professional intervention? However, perhaps a more serious aspect of the problem lies in disagreements, some of them at a fundamental level, about the purpose of community development. These are often expressed in terms of the contrast between, on the one hand, community development as a campaigning activity, part of the tradition of social movements globally and, on the other, community development as an intervention, helping to ensure that local people have opportunities to participate as well as to be supported. Historically, this disagreement rests on the duality of community development as a social movement and a profession.

Core themes

When reflecting on the history of professional community development interventions, we discover a variety of reasons for interventions, the theories that justify them and the methods used to implement them. There are significant differences, too, in the history of these interventions as far as their direction and emphases are concerned. The range is wide: socio-cultural development, community education, the fight against poverty/exclusion, social/community planning, social action, pressure groups, community-based economic development, multicultural mediation, civil society development. Even the term used to refer to community development varies from country to country – community action, community organisation, community social work, community work, social-cultural animation. There are some countries where the word 'community' as an adjective is used with hesitation or not used at all, either because there is simply no word for it (as in Sweden), or because the word has negative historical connotations (as in Germany).

What does the elasticity of these interventions mean? Is it an intangible diffusion, something that renders the formation of a profession impossible; or is it the opposite, an inexhaustible richness and strength? The picture is given even greater shades of complexity by the evidence that community development is both a social movement and a profession at the same time.

We can talk about community development only if members of a community themselves, their groups, organisations and institutions, develop their own community. It is not the community development worker who develops the community but the community that develops itself. The community development worker acts as a catalyst and provides professional support in this process. He or she will often initiate contact and activities in order to encourage a community to take over an initiative. In this way community-based solutions are sought, a process that is then supported by the community development worker with the help of various empowerment tools. A good community development process is a movement in which residents, who become increasingly active, seek ways of contributing to the improvement of the community's quality of life and create their own organisations and cooperative structures. During the process, there are always new individuals and groups who become active as a result of either criticising the process or of offering an alternative; these community 'players' will invariably create new situations, thus changing the planning, decision-making and control mechanisms.

The phenomenon of a movement or process provides great strength but at the same time, due to its specific nature, it makes representation, the creation of a common image and external communication more difficult. Working with a movement is not necessarily characterised by deep and long-term commitments, and citizens' involvement can come down simply to saying 'yes' or 'no'. It is also true that response times are unpredictable; there are examples of sudden, immediate actions and examples of step-by-step development or processes that slow down, almost to stagnation, then unexpectedly regain momentum.

Some elements of working with a process can be criticised for being inefficient or parochial. We should remember, however, that we are talking about building civil society as a counter to the state and the concentration of excessive power. People become involved both to reduce or eliminate deficiencies and to propose alternatives. All of this, for good reasons, takes time. A community is always changing and this means that it is difficult for an outsider to follow and interpret the processes that are taking place. Yet the essence of all community development lies precisely in this continuous, ongoing phenomenon of movement and change. Be it locality development, social planning or social action, the element of process is always apparent.

Community development, irrespective of the term used to refer to it, involves working not only with local people, community groups and organisations but also at regional, national and international levels. A key question to explore is the basis on which such wide-ranging activity can be regarded as a profession. Certainly, the direction and social functions of this specialist area provide a reassuring identity.

Community development activity always focuses on increasing the participation of those involved with issues. In terms of its social functions, self-help, cooperation and community activity aimed at changing existing circumstances are present in all the community functions that will be discussed later.

On the one hand, community activity is directed at people in need. On the other hand, it is achieved through the strength of communities identifying and publicly articulating their needs themselves. It is directed at reforms, at influencing decision making and legislation, placing the emphasis on change, not simply on adaptation. There is a strong preventative theme in community development. It is able to enhance the strengths that are inherent in communities and to organise communication and solidarity among people. It can help communities to organise – self-help, interest and identity representation and pressure groups – and encourage them to engage with the new institutions of civil society. Community development can help excluded people and marginalised social groups to articulate their interests and to recognise, identify and confront the social institutions and groups that prevent them from representing those interests (Henderson, 2005).

When communities act together there is motivation for education and learning; it opens up closed worlds, it widens spheres of activities. It creates new organisations, establishing links between them and helping citizens and their communities to use the institutions that have been created for them.

Community development has become an activity that contributes to social integration and community cohesion. It is able to increase civil society's potential to take initiatives and action. It is able to help the transformation or re-establishment of society's institutional systems; it can bring together the various interests in society and build partnerships at both regional and society-wide levels. Finally, it can increase society's capacity for democratic self-organisation.

The Hungarian Association of Community Development (HACD) takes the view that a profession needs to justify itself in three main areas: identity, philosophy and strategy.

- Professional identity includes professionals' own opinions of the aims of their profession and how they justify its existence. Community development workers tend to argue that their profession is key to achieving social change because of the involvement of local people; it can develop participative democracy; it can encourage small-scale, self-reliant and self-organising communities; it can contribute to the development of community-based institutions designed to create sustainable systems. Professional community development workers will also usually include in their definition their links with other professions, notably planning, youth work, adult education and social work.
- The philosophy of a profession is the conceptual framework that places the identity of that profession into a broader system of ideas. Does the profession have stated objectives and goals such as the attainment of a 'good society', a modern community and sustainable development? What are the points of contact with related disciplines such as sociology, philosophy, social policy and social psychology and with communication, culture and sub-cultural theory, solidarity, the

notion of underclass, conflict? These disciplines provide a framework for self-reflection in community development. The question is not only what the profession wants to achieve but also why it strives to achieve it. The theoretical framework of the profession changes because it is in the nature of community development to shift in response to social change. The 'whys' give the answer in terms of professional values and principles, which are the most important indicators of professional activity.

• Finally, professional legitimacy also requires an established and continually expanding professional strategy. In other words, it needs to take into account recognised practice and the application of professional procedures, ensuring their continual development.

In an era of constant change, professions cannot be examined in traditional ways. Ultimately, we have to face the theoretical and methodological pluralism of community development, and the fact that this stems from the nature of community development itself.

The extensive borders of the profession are worth viewing as a resource for enrichment that requires interdisciplinarity and professional 'cross-border' cooperation in order to manage complex social problems. These may include cooperation in areas such as public administration, government policies, community education, adult education, social work, environmental protection, architecture and local and regional development.

Should community development be an independent profession or should it be part of other professions? There are many examples of how within, for example, the framework of social work, community development can be narrowed down to a service-providing activity instead of working for development and change. We can also see how, in central and eastern Europe, it is being used as a tool in the new regional development profession, focusing predominantly on infrastructural development and treating the principle of involving stakeholders as a formality.

If community development becomes subordinate to any other profession, there is a risk that it might lose its interdisciplinary character and independence, and different interest groups will use it as a means to achieve their own goals. Community development is a contributory type of profession; on its own it is incapable of solving social problems. However, through its specific tools and by complementing the tools of other professions, it can effectively contribute to solving problems. Professions with low social prestige tend to struggle for their legitimacy and for recognition as independent disciplines and as recognised and supported professions. If part of the essence of community development lies in its interdisciplinarity and contributory nature, we can see that it is these two ideas that explain why, in a world of increasing specialisation, gaining legitimacy is particularly difficult.

Origins and growth

The emergence of community development as a professional field tells us that the growth of the profession can be linked directly to democracy and the emergence and development of civil society. Participation – the most important community development principle – will only be realised if community activity emerges from the needs of those involved and there is empowerment from the grassroots upwards. This democratic notion cannot work, or can only work in a limited way, in authoritarian or pseudo-democratic systems, such as under state socialism. As we shall see, the same applies to the other principles of the profession.

The internationalism of community development is embedded in its past. One commentator goes so far as to state that:

> From an international perspective, it is clear that community development has been one of the most significant social forces in the process of planned change. (Campfens, 1997, p 20)

Over the past 100 years, examples of community development initiatives, programmes and policies can be found in many countries as well as within international agencies. The British government used the idea of community development as part of its colonial policy. In the 1930s, Saul Alinsky, the radical American community organiser, mobilised people in Chicago to improve their living conditions. With these two examples we witness again the duality that is evident within community development: on the one hand, its use by government and official bodies as a means of reaching out to communities, on the other, the phenomenon of social movements that use community development as an organising principle. In the following historical summary of community development in different regions of the world, we refer to only a few of the many examples that come into these two categories as well as to examples that bridge them.

Western Europe

The western European experience of community development has been dominated by initiatives and practice in the UK. This began with the work of the settlements in London's East End at the beginning of the last century and was sustained by the experiences of rent strikes during the First World War. From the late 1940s, one strand of community development in Britain took the form of setting up and supporting community centres on new council estates and in new towns. The other main strand was the interest of key individuals, many of whom had seen the potential of community development when working as colonial administrators, in applying the idea in the UK context. It was from here that the beginnings of a literature on community development emerged. During the 1950s, this was informed by experiences and ideas from North America, particularly the writing of Murray Ross (1955).

Following a number of voluntary sector initiatives in the mid-1960s, it is generally agreed that community development in the UK came of age in 1968 (see Henderson, 2008). That year saw the publication of influential reports and the emergence of government funding for community development, including the launch of 12 Community Development Projects. Subsequently, community development experienced a period of expansion in the social work context. However, when social work began to distance itself from community development, the latter came to be associated increasingly with economic issues. In the 1980s, the radical market-oriented changes introduced by the Conservative government threatened to leave community development in a state of confusion. This was compounded by the effects of the economic recession towards the end of the decade. Yet community development survived this period in British politics and rebuilt itself. From the early 1990s, the identities of community development in Scotland, Northern Ireland, England and Wales began to become more distinctive. This has been reinforced in Scotland and Wales following devolution. The 1997–2007 Blair governments reaffirmed the partnership dimension within the underlying economic context for community development and this continued under the government of Gordon Brown.

Murray Ross's view that community work should be understood as one of three social work methods (case work, group work and community work) was picked up in continental Europe, particularly France where community work was, intermittently, present within both the social work and adult education professions. Elsewhere in Europe, professional community development emerged later than in the UK, the Netherlands and France (de Wit, 1997). From the early 1970s, it gained a significant toehold in the Netherlands and the Flemish part of Belgium. It was linked closely with urban renewal. In both countries, community development went on to become recognised as a profession. Strong links were made between Dutch and British community development trainers and practitioners. There was also ongoing contact between British and Irish trainers and practitioners. Ireland, too, had long-standing experiences of community development, particularly in rural areas and through the work of Muintir na Tire.

At the beginning of the 1990s, community development organisations from nine European countries set up an organisation in order to share ideas and information. Called the Combined European Bureau for Social Development (CEBSD), this organisation later expanded its membership, notably with the addition of HACD, and evolved into more of a network than an organisation. This enabled it to make contact with a wide range of traditions and experiences from the cooperative movement in Italy to adult education groups in Scandinavia.

Central and eastern Europe

The collapse of communism in central and eastern Europe at the end of the 1980s opened the way for the emergence of community development. Many of the initiatives have been small-scale and hesitant but, as we shall see, it is in this region that clear connections between civil society and community development can be made. At the same time, it is important to note that the central and eastern European region also has a tradition of community development. Self-help and mutual help groups, associations, secular and church charities, philanthropic organisations, intellectuals, reformers and the workers' movement all strived for social progress.

The region has had the progressive elements typical of the development of modern communities. One could find many good examples to illustrate community movements and organised interventions. However, because of a lack of a comprehensive democratic social system, the movements and interventions have exerted less political influence – on social policy, legislation and sponsorship practices – than in the older democracies. Modern solutions appeared more as an exception or as experiments, not as widely applied practice. The region's history had relatively few large-scale grassroots organisations and social movements. In addition, the region has not had the techniques and professions supported by membership organisations.

HACD is unusual in that it was perhaps closest to the philanthropic traditions of intellectuals who, in the mid-1970s, were searching for new forms of modernisation and democratisation. Similar motivations inspired Székelyföldi Közösségfejlesztők Egyesülete (Community Development Association for the Székely-Hungarian Region of Transylvania, Romania) when it started its activities two decades later. There was also a trace of the intellectual's sense of mission in the formation of Associatia Romana de Dezvoltare Comunitara (Romanian Association for Community Development) in 1999 and Centrum Wspierania Aktywnosci Lokalnej (Centres for Local Activity) in Poland in 2000.

Otherwise, the emergence of community development organisations in the region tended to be helped more by external inspiration and support than by organic efforts. Funding bodies emerged as organisations for institution building and development in central and eastern Europe. Yet to what extent can societies incorporate the social improvement efforts of these organisations? Organisations that have evolved as a result of organic development tend to have a higher level of acceptance than their newer, externally established counterparts.

A special feature of many community development organisations in the region is their strong link to cultural houses. These resource and meeting centres are equivalent to the community centres found in many parts of western Europe. The Hungarian, Romanian and Polish organisations have direct contact with this type of institution, although they are at different phases in the history of this relationship. The Polish organisation encourages those working in cultural houses to learn and use a particular community development method, while members of the Hungarian and Romanian organisations began by reforming the work carried out in these institutions and using this as a basis for gradually reaching a wider social spectrum and creating an interdisciplinary profession.

Community development in Hungary developed from community education. This profession was meant to fill the void left by people's own initiatives. These had existed but were banned during the decades of the soviet-type dictatorship. The community education profession was centred on the cultural houses. Following the 1956 revolution, activities in these centres were characterised by decreasing political learning and increased cultural and leisure content.

Community development in Hungary also evolved from settlement-type activities and ideas in the mid-1970s – meeting places and centres for use by local people. An experiment called 'Open House' was launched with the aim of raising the profile and appeal of the network of cultural houses, a network that was well organised in towns and villages but largely neglected by residents. This action research, carried out in 20 towns and villages over a period of several years, highlighted residents' needs and provided organised community-based cultural responses to those needs (Varga, 1975). While the results of the experiment were promising, most of the population still kept themselves away from community life. As a result, those taking the initiative decided to move away from the focus on cultural houses in order to engage with people who would not or could not get involved. The first community development initiatives in Hungary began with conversations that took place with local people in their homes. This form of communication gave opportunities for those visited to introduce themselves and put their problems into words, thus providing encouragement for meeting with others. A common feature of both the settlement house type of activity and community development is that, in contrast to an institutional approach, they take people as their starting point. The early settlement and community development activities were both characterised by strong values.

When examining the historical background of the profession outside Hungary, we can see that it was often in settlement houses that the first community development workers tested out professional intervention methods and, more importantly, the direction of community development. Rather than focusing on adaptation, they placed the emphasis on generating change. In the settlement houses, they did not teach people how to put up with the existing conditions but enabled those involved to handle change. Their activity was development work rather than service provision.

While the logic behind the emergence of the community development profession shows highly similar features in western Europe as well as in Hungary and other central and eastern European countries, it is important to be aware of significant differences in motivations and professional views. In terms of ideological history, the origins of community development in central and eastern Europe go back to the intellectual's perception of the philanthropic educational movement of the Enlightenment. This, it was felt, was motivated by the sense of mission needed to advance a nation. This role of the intellectual has significant historical traditions, whether we look at Hungarian, Polish, Czech or Russian examples.

Intellectuals had a long-held belief that they had to 'raise the people up' by acting as a kind of bridge between the more developed and less developed parts of society, between the democratic, free world and the semi-feudal one. Given the existence of both a substantial bourgeoisie and a working class, they could see no alternative. It was not wealth that formed the background to an intellectual's perception of his or her role in social activity, but education, an insight into both the national context and a different world – and a desire to narrow the gap. A philanthropic person could be a simple village priest, a wealthy landowner or factory manager. Today we can look on them as our early ancestors in community development. Their role, because of the different social context, has no negative connotations attached to it. They wanted a free and educated nation and a modernised economy and society. In their bid to improve society, they were sometimes forced to sacrifice wealth and lifestyle. Their activities were not aimed at maintaining the status quo but at encouraging progress and change.

The perception of the intellectual's role that emerged during the Enlightenment changed over time, especially in terms of its social role. At different periods, the role was perceived as a free-floating intellectual, an onlooker, an outsider, a supervisor, an insider or an expresser of independent opinion, a social critic, a provider of information, a mediator or a helper. The role also changed during the time of state socialism, mainly on the basis of Gramsci's intelligentsia theory:

> The way of life for the new intelligentsia cannot be comprised of eloquence, which is an external and momentary engine of emotions and passions, but of active involvement in practical life as a builder, an organiser.... It should shift from technique as work to technique as a humanist view of history, without which we will remain 'specialists' and fail to become 'leaders' (specialist + politician). (Huszár, 1975, p 48)

This view had a direct influence on the formation of Hungarian public education and community development. A direct predecessor of Hungarian community development can be seen in the education of intellectuals at the Budapest Technical University, the essence of which was to involve future intellectuals in practical life. Two movements developed from the intellectuals' ideas in 1970–73: the 'University students for public education' and the 'Winter public education exercise' movements. In the former, university students undertook voluntary work in the preparation of the technical drawings and refurbishment plans for 200 cultural houses in Hungary. In the public education practice, study groups were organised by students of various professions (engineers, doctors, teachers, lawyers, economists) from the country's major higher education institutions. They spent two weeks in several local communities studying the lives of the inhabitants. They wrote summaries of their experiences and these were presented to the host communities and the universities involved (Varga and Verceg, 1998).

This emphasis on the role of the intellectual has, of course, been refined and changed over the past 20-30 years. However, those committed to community development are still motivated by a sense of mission. This perspective will remain important until new citizens become strong and go through a process of democratisation. It is the slow development of democracy that still allows philanthropic and intellectually driven ideas to hold sway.

During the period 2000–05, with the help of Charity Know How, the Mott Foundation and the Soros Foundation, HACD organised an 'East–East' collaboration project among the Bulgarian, Czech, Polish, Hungarian, Romanian, Romanian-Hungarian, Russian, Slovak and Ukrainian community development organisations. This cooperation revealed two types of community development approach, existing side by side:

- One approach sees community development as a broad social reform concept and method; these are the organisations that have come to community development as a result of the type of organic development mentioned earlier.
- The other approach is represented by a new generation whose organisations have been set up by foreign funding agencies. They follow the more modern role of technical assistance.

Examples of programmes that have been run using the second approach demonstrate that it would not be easy to secure the long-term acceptance and internalisation of this type of role – sustained development – even with significant external professional support. The reasons for this are to be found in the democratic deficit in the region as well as in the fact that the supporting role has not yet really become part of the culture, even if the deficits it aims to address are clearly present. The newly and externally formed organisations are experiencing many failures and are in the process of realising that this work also requires knowledge of local culture and society in order to gain social acceptance and cooperation.

North America

Community development obtained a high profile in the US in the 1960s and 1970s as part of the government's War on Poverty. It was supported by research, training and some impressive literature that focused increasingly on social planning and community organisation (see Kramer and Specht, 1969). There was extensive debate on the relationship between neighbourhood organising and established institutions, prompted to some extent by the legislative requirement for citizen participation in planning and decision making. There were significant shifts in the focus and terms of community action:

> Organisers work now on a broader set of issues, using more varied, sophisticated strategies. Most striking is the erosion of boundaries separating conventional community organising from coalition-building and electoral politics. (Miller et al, 1995, p 112)

Many activists and community organisers who had been involved in opposing American involvement in Vietnam in the 1960s, challenging racial discrimination and combating poverty – summarised by Specht as a concern with organising the unaffiliated and the development of neighbourhood organisations – became more pragmatic. Community action became increasingly linked with community enterprise and community banking, both of which were driven forward by government, local government and the private sector. Interestingly, Kraushaar and colleagues, in commenting on five American case studies, note that there has been a shift away from domination by government organisations and a return towards grassroots approaches. They also identify a growing realisation among federal programmers of the need to have locally designed goals and strategies (Kraushaar et al, 1999).

Increasing emphasis has been placed in the US on community capacity building and an asset-based approach to community development (Kretzmann and McKnight, 1993). At the same time, ways of combining socioeconomic and environmental strategies within a community development framework are being explored. Similar processes have taken place in Canada where community economic development has a well-established tradition, particularly in eastern Nova Scotia where practitioners trace their heritage back to the Antigonish Movement – a movement of cooperatives and adult education that began in the region in the 1930s (MacAulay, 2001). During the 1990s, there were lively debates in Canada on where community development was going – or being taken. On the one hand, there was a strong desire to work with the most marginalised groups in society as well as to encourage health and social work agencies to adopt community development strategies. On the other hand, there was evidence of rifts developing between professionals and activists, particularly in Québec where there is also significant experience of community economic development.

We could have drawn attention to the emergence of community development in a number of other countries in the developed world, notably South Africa, Australia, New Zealand and Hong Kong. Our intention, however, is not to provide a 'Cook's tour' of community development worldwide but rather to convey a sense of community development's breadth and depth. It is remarkable how core ideas and principles have been applied in very contrasting social, economic and political contexts, usually with minimal resources. The language used to describe and analyse it may vary, and different emphases are placed on component parts – leadership and accountability, for example – but its essence is always recognisable.

Southern countries

We conclude our historical summary by referring to the significance of community development thinking and experiences in southern countries, most especially the work of the Brazilian adult educationalist Paulo Freire. The impact of his book *Pedagogy of the oppressed* (1972) has been widespread. It speaks to the concerns of activists, professional community development workers, trainers and theorists, and his warning about the dangers of action without reflection remains of paramount importance. Issues of the *Community Development Journal* and conferences organised by the International Association for Community Development confirm the extent to which community development has become rooted in many southern countries. As in other regions, we can observe the dual purposes to which it has been put: underpinning a wide range of local, regional and national social movements while at the same time forming part of government and other agencies' social, economic and environmental programmes.

During the 1990s, the idea of partnership between northern and southern non-governmental organisations (NGOs) came under scrutiny because it was seen to maintain the power of northern NGOs as funders of southern ones. Today, good practice of northern NGOs such as ActionAid and Oxfam is to almost always channel resources to southern countries through voluntary and community groups based in villages and neighbourhoods. Increasingly, southern NGOs 'began to set their own agendas and to develop research, policy, and advocacy capacities' (Pearce, 2000, p 25). There is now widespread recognition of the variety of ways in which participation has been developed in southern countries and of the need to support different approaches as well as learn from them. There is increasing interest in both South–South and South–North as well as North–North and North–South learning. Community development, after many years of struggle, trial and error and debates, is a central part of this development.

Growing awareness of the significance and potential of community development, in northern and southern countries, is a constant theme of this historical review. An historical perspective on community development is important not only because it enables us to learn from past successes and failures but also because it helps us to gauge the condition of community development today. It enables us to identify patterns and trends. It is also essential for being able to understand the values, theories and methods of community development. This, as we shall see in the following chapters, is a challenging undertaking. Community development is not a defined, tidy profession. Its growth has been uneven and it is spread across an array of issues and disciplines. Analysis of its current and future problems and challenges can, however, be based on solid foundations.

FOUR

Socialisation

Socialisation means the understanding of a culture and its norms and how one either lives within a culture or challenges it. It is not a concept that is given much attention today in the West, mainly because of its association with the American functional tradition of sociology and the latter's perceived failure to address issues of gender, race and class within the framework of socialisation. The sociologist Roland Warren, however, locates his writing on socialisation within a strong community context: and, as explained in Chapter Two, we are using his community model as the conceptual framework for Chapters Four to Eight.

> Although the community is not the only system actively involved in the socialisation of the individual, it is ... the arena in which the individual is confronted with the particular way in which his or her society structures individual behaviour. (Warren, 1963, p 174)

It is the community perspective on socialisation that informs this chapter. The topic does not figure much in community development literature. It is important, therefore, to appreciate why it has significance in central and eastern Europe. The starting point is the democratic deficit and lack of solidarity that are on the political agendas of all European countries, but the problems in the new European democracies present themselves in a more direct way than in the old democracies. This chapter focuses on dilemmas and practice in the central and eastern European region and traces the capacity in Hungary to link socialisation with community development.

While there are significant differences across the region, practice is similar and trends and patterns can be identified. What stands out is the struggle to achieve meaningful social and cultural change. 'Transition from one type of culture to another' is how Attila Gergely, a Hungarian sociologist, describes the shift needed as a consequence of the systemic change resulting from the regime change. The key question concerns the pace at which central and eastern European societies can adjust. The uneasy social atmosphere, lack of confidence, frustration, low levels of social participation and still lower citizen participation are all factors that indicate what Gergely refers to as the deficit of a whole culture and the failure of its 're-culturing' processes (Gergely, 1991, p 4).

The high expectations and ever-worsening failures of the post-revolutionary period since the end of the 1990s have shown that, without being socialised to democracy, a market economy and a European identity, communities can only renew and reorganise themselves slowly. Democracy can only be developed and managed by people who have been prepared and empowered to do so.

Community development and community-based learning

The community development process is essentially about empowerment. It is not the community development worker who empowers people but the learning process taking place through community initiatives and community action. To enable democratic thinking and active citizenship to spread more rapidly, it is not enough simply to increase the number of free adult training programmes and organise them into a regularly and securely functioning system.

It is essential for community development to engage with the socialisation process of children and young people. Programmes that combine early socialisation and community development focus on interactive learning and consist of informal elements complemented by formal learning. Living in a community must be practised even with the youngest age groups. In addition to single actions such as special days or outings, it is also necessary to work and learn together.

Good practice in community development has shown that, with professional assistance, children and young people are able to set collective objectives and tasks and to organise in ways that fit with contemporary norms and fashions. There is a wealth of evidence internationally to support this contention (see Hart, 1997). In the UK, work over a number of years by advocacy groups such as the Children's Rights Alliance for England and by children's organisations such as Save the Children has kept the issue of children's participation on the national agenda. It has also informed local community development practice. The 1989 United Nations (UN) Convention on the Rights of the Child includes important clauses on children's right to participate in society: to be involved, to be part of decisions as well as to be consulted. It provides a useful platform on which to argue for the theme of children and community development, above all in the context of sustainable development. Environmental mismanagement has a severe impact on children's safety, health, mobility and development. Work with and on behalf of children and young people has been a significant part of community development in the UK for many years. Adults' concern for children and their future has often been the springboard for community action, especially around the need for safe play areas. The social context, however, in which community development with children takes place today has changed out of all recognition from the past. Widespread anxieties about putting children at risk means that considerable care has to be taken when any action is planned. Yet the Convention on the Rights of the Child can still be used as an anchor point for community development

Local curricula

The process of community socialisation can be made more effective through complementing the core national educational curriculum with local curricula developed in communities, thereby giving the national curriculum legitimacy in the locality. The main elements of a local curriculum can be:

- community studies, the socialisation aspects of the local development plan and the development of a community-based economic culture in the early stages of socialisation;
- learning about democracy in school and everyday life.

These need to be embedded in an adequate practice within the school system and the community.

Implementation of local curricula is not the exclusive responsibility of schools but concerns the community as a whole. The catalyst can be either the school or the community development professionals it has involved, but the process cannot be effective without the cooperation of parents, local institutions and local residents. People need to be aware of the process and be encouraged to own it themselves. The socialisation efforts of the school in the area of community and democracy will be futile if actual situations keep contradicting them. In the new European Union (EU) member states, students learn on the basis of EU-compatible curricula, so that the legal framework exists for stakeholders to organise good schools locally. However, this is seldom the case in alienated local societies where non-collective and non-democratic thinking is dominant. Hence, in almost all localities community development professionals are needed who are empowered by the local authority or a school to help integrate and harmonise the socialisation process inside or outside a particular institution.

Familiarity with the local community has to be continually enriched and enhanced. This includes familiarity with aspects of local history, traditions, knowledge and experience, as well as with the local landscape and nature, the built environment, industry, market and service systems and public life. Last but not least, citizens have to be in an active relationship with these systems. The purpose of community studies is for stakeholders to learn about a range of issues and needs that are present in a given locality, while also having a vision for the future that involves them in an active role. A school and a community should deal not only with the past but also with the issues that people face today. Young people must develop an understanding of the basic 'drivers' of society and the potential for action. These range from organising life in a way mostly determined by the outside world to local development controlled by local communities; from unemployment to career opportunities; and from local minority groups and human rights issues to the responsibilities of an active citizen.

Implementation of local development plans often proves to be problematic. The proposed action often assumes skills and capacities on the part of citizens that are not present in a given locality. For example, one of the main requisites for developing local tourism is residents' familiarity with their own community, the communication and language skills of local people, local businesses and the knowledge that programme leaders have of their area. Unless these competencies are incorporated into the local curriculum, community members will not be able to implement their plans. The same can be said about bio-agriculture and ecological farming. Both of these are popular but they are practised successfully by only a few people. In this respect, natural and environmental awareness that involves familiarity with the local natural environment must be complemented by special farming studies and skills.

Local development plans must build not only on people's willingness to set up enterprises but also on their related knowledge. The development of an economic culture is one of the most crucial challenges in the central and eastern European region. Community development can contribute significantly to community-based economic development and we examine this in the next chapter. Here we touch on some of the community examples of early socialisation that relate to this theme.

Examples

- In the Hungarian village of Szegvár (population 5,000), residents of all age groups demonstrated an unusually strong community identity and commitment during a community development exercise that took place in 2003–04. Only later did the development worker solve the mystery of this unprecedented activity: it emerged that, from the mid-1980s, students at the local school had been given lessons on their local community and in 1993 the school board decided that every student over nine years of age should study the history of the local community. The subject was named 'local studies' and the curriculum and a study book called *The story of the Szegvár area* were developed by one of the teachers. The book contained the history and ethnography of the local community, as well as information on the locality. The local syllabus was incorporated into the subjects of biology and geography and into children's leisure programmes, where they produced traditional pottery, collected old artefacts, carried out interviews with elderly people and so on. The teachers committed to the local curriculum say that it is not enough to have a committed teacher, a good study book or even practical experiences; the positive and supportive attitude of the local community is also indispensable for effective education. The school has managed to win over the parents to the cause, and the local newspaper reports on the work regularly. In this way, being a Szegvár resident has become a public matter affecting the whole community (Kovács, 2007).

- In Denmark, production schools provide a community-based, optional one-year programme that prepares young people aged 16–19 to set up and work in community enterprises. The production school system was developed in 1985 but its roots reach back to the 19th century, when the first folk high schools came into existence. This kind of school is usually set up by local communities in order to tackle youth unemployment. A production school produces and distributes goods and services in response to circumstances, and young people are trained in production and service activities. The products of a given production school reflect the demands of the community where it is located. Most Danish production schools employ young people in the areas of landscape design, metalwork and carpentry, household and textile products and handicrafts. However, new programmes have been started in the areas of ecology and tourism, electronic data processing and new technology. Some schools offer foreign study trips and theoretical training in order to prepare young people for the tourism industry. Practical training is undertaken in the community where the school is located.

- Several European community education programmes have been developed to train young people through participation and prepare them for choosing a career. In 1990, for example, the International Community Education Association (ICEA) organised a conference in Berlin entitled 'Learning through productive action'. The conference led to the establishment of the Institute for Productive Learning in Europe (IPLE), which has organised a number of programmes including an initiative supported by the EU's Social Fund on youth enterprises and enterprise learning. The programmes emphasise the involvement of young people in their own socialisation processes – self-determination rather than 'being done to'. The programmes help young people who are considered a potential threat to society by allowing them to demonstrate their inventiveness and creativity towards older generations. IPLE also set up the International Network of Productive Schools, a cooperative that involves over 40 institutions and projects from 16 different countries. In one of the workshops at the 1995 ICEA conference, participants planned a 'Take your Café – Build your Future' programme that has been implemented in several European countries. Within the framework of this programme, cooperative or associative youth cafés were established with help from the local partners involved in the programme. For example, between 1996 and 1999, 14 'school firms' and three youth cafés were established in Berlin.

- Community development professionals in Hungary developed an experimental curriculum for training young people. It was introduced in the technical school of Kunszentmiklós, a small Hungarian town with 8,000 inhabitants. The aim of the curriculum was to promote both community-based economic development and an underlying economic culture through developing the cognitive, analytical, planning and implementation skills of students. Although the programme, funded by the Soros Foundation, achieved some minor successes, it did not result in a significant breakthrough. This was because the school's senior managers were not interested in assisting the process and only passively tolerated the presence of the community development professional (Mészáros, 1999). Training programmes that train teachers to develop entrepreneurial skills are essential. The main community development-related content of these courses is familiarity with the local community, the consideration of traditional handcrafts, local products and special local services, the development of self-confidence and a community vision, and preparing people for cooperation.

The so-called minority curriculum must also be part of local curricula. The need to include minority studies in educational schemes became evident after the post-1989 democratic transformation in relation to two main issues: can a mother tongue be re-acquired and can traditions be revived? A local perspective on education allows for the introduction of minority studies that synthesises subjects such as the language and culture of a particular minority and its role in forming history and culture, minority and civil rights, and so on. According to the Hungarian national core curriculum approved in 1995, the special objective of minority studies is to preserve and strengthen minority identity. Croatian, German, Romanian, Slovakian and Slovenian minority studies exist in the public education system, albeit not as a compulsory element. In Poland, minority nursery schools and primary schools have been offering education in the minority language for a number of years and the training of minority teachers has been included in teacher training schemes.

In theory, the provision of minority studies is in harmony with recommendations regarding the education rights of national minorities issued by the Organisation for Security and Co-operation in Europe. However, the complaints and appeals received by minority ombudsmen suggest shortcomings in the legal measures and practice, mostly in connection with the Roma minority. Only a small number of schools in central and eastern Europe have Roma studies in their curriculum. Study materials provided centrally (books, audiovisual study packs, bibliographies and so on) are also lacking. Accordingly, teaching is heavily dependent on each individual's access to resources. This is just one of a number of challenges facing the development of socialisation programmes.

Active citizenship

Besides organising classroom activities on democracy, one way of accelerating the process of democratisation is for teachers and students of educational institutions to develop local community development programmes for active citizenship and participation, with the help of professional community development organisations. These programmes should cover the whole schooling period, and even the pre-school period. Local children and young people's councils, for example, have the scope to take on responsibilities and undertake decision making, provided that they retain their independence. These were pioneered in France in the early 1990s and have subsequently become widely recognised throughout Europe. The initiatives in France stimulated Hungarian community development professionals to develop a Hungarian version, while in the UK it is usual for local authorities to support children and young people's councils. The report of the Advisory Group on Education for Citizenship and the Teaching of Democracy in Schools (1998) – the Crick report – was significant in that it raised the profile of the issue of citizenship and young people. Citizenship education was introduced into the school curriculum in 2002.

The experience of Bezenye, a village in north-west Hungary, illustrates how children and young people can become involved in local governance. Here, the local authority took a lead role in bringing young people together, listening to their ideas and supporting plans and programmes initiated and organised by the young people themselves. The children and young people's council is composed of ten representatives and a mayor. They are elected democratically and anonymously by young people in the community. The council publishes a local newsletter, organises programmes and summer camps, takes part in the preservation and improvement of the local environment, runs a youth information and counselling bureau, attends all local authority sessions where decisions concerning young people are made and organises training courses on democracy and the EU.

It may be argued that this kind of local democratic activity by children and young people only scratches the surface of participation – a tame, even conservative, attempt to engage with children and young people. In most countries there tends to be an over-representation of middle-class children on children and young people's councils. There is, however, much variation in how children and young people's councils have been set up and, crucially, much depends on the social and political context in any one country. In most central and eastern European nations, the interest of government and local government in supporting children and young people's councils is important precisely because such councils can be a basic building block on which other, more radical, initiatives can be based. Councils also provide a sense of continuity and an acceptance that the involvement of children and young people in democratic organisation and decision making needs to be long-lasting. The same argument applies in the context of the UK and other western European countries. Children and young people's councils form part of a continuum of programmes undertaken with children and young people that can be supported by community development.

—

Community schools and community education

Community schools are set up to meet the needs of local communities through supporting and coordinating citizen initiatives. Such schools are based on the philosophy of community education, involving the community in enriching the education of children for the sake of developing individuals, families and society. Community education is a process that assumes that each member of a community is entitled to become involved in articulating the needs of that community and ensuring that local institutions cooperate with community members.

Networks of community schools are active in many countries. Community schools began to develop in the US, following an initiative by the Charles Stewart Mott Foundation in the 1930s. In Israel, a network of community schools was established in 1978 within the national elementary school system. The schools use local curricula, organise joint training courses for parents and teachers and initiate and support local community development schemes. There is a long and rich tradition of community schools and colleges in the UK, from the inspirational work of Henry Morris in Cambridgeshire through a multiplicity of experiments in both urban and rural settings. They have offered significant, if little noticed, opportunities for community development. When schools employed community development workers, the aim was to help the schools reach out to the communities in which they were located and to encourage community use of school buildings. Over the past 20 years, the sense of excitement about community schools has waned; over the same period, opportunities for connecting community development with informal adult education have declined significantly.

Community schools were first established in Hungary in 1993 with funding from the Mott Foundation and the Soros Foundation. Besides introducing training programmes, the schools have organised family and environmental programmes and have also forged links with local social and cultural institutions and civil society organisations. With the ending of the grant period, the key question is whether this type of institution can be embedded in Hungarian society and gain the support of local authorities and other social actors.

In Romania, a community schools programme is run under the name 'active community school' and has been adjusted to the Romanian context on the basis of the Danish model. This type of school is often referred to as the 'democracy school'. It uses its own community as the basis for the curriculum and also provides a focal point for local community life and involvement in public affairs. In

2004, the Romanian Association for Community Development hosted its central and eastern European partners within the framework of the East–East programme of the Soros Foundation. Participants visited a rural community school and witnessed children teaching their parents and grandparents how to use a computer.

Eco-schools

Eco-schools can contribute to the development of local identity based on familiarity with the local community, the development of environmental awareness and the formation of local environmental movements. The following objectives of eco-schools demonstrate the extent to which they invariably form part of a community development programme:

- new alliances are made between the school and the local community within the framework of regional development;
- there is a shift of emphasis in educational policies from teaching to learning;
- foundations are laid for lifelong learning;
- the school becomes embedded in a learning society;
- learning motives and strategies are formed and strengthened;
- the school itself becomes a learning organisation;
- digital communication and the internet can become part of the development process as a means of managing local learning.

Eco-schools emerged in Europe in the 1990s. As well as undertaking environmental training, they are a key driver in the development of schools and learning. Hungary became part of the movement in 2000, initially with 50 and today with around 200 schools. These schools collaborate at the national level and their activities even cover day nurseries. The fact that the pattern has been adapted extensively does not necessarily imply that the approach can easily be put into practice. The proliferation of such schools does not necessarily mean that they achieve their aims easily. The same principle applies to eco-schools as to children and young people's councils and community schools – they can only maintain their original objectives inasmuch as the culture of the local actors (school, parents and the local community) implementing those objectives is community-centred and democratic.

The Environment and School Initiatives (ENSI) programme and its network development programme, School Development through Environmental Education, were both established by the Organisation for Economic Co-operation and Development's Centre for Education, Research and Innovation in order to promote cooperation and learning exchange among schools, teacher training institutions and educational authorities. UN member states have acknowledged the period 2005–15 as the Decade of Learning for Sustainability. This has inspired ENSI to work with UNESCO, the coordinating agency for this sustainability initiative, to develop a myriad of related programmes (Havas and Varga, 2006; see also www.ensi.org).

Among European community development organisations, it is the Norwegian Stiftelsen Idébanken (Ideas Bank), set up in 1991, which has demonstrated most effectively the connections between community development, environmental protection and sustainable development. The Ideas Bank has concentrated on developing the involvement of local communities in planning their future. It uses a particular method called dialogue workshop to do this. It is also active in the area of organising public debates and campaigns, and influencing national politics. The organisation runs a 'Future centre' in Oslo with a public library as well as exhibitions and audiovisual presentations introducing local community initiatives organised within the framework of Local Agenda 21, the UN programme for implementing sustainable development at the local level. It also helps community groups and local council representatives to develop and enhance opportunities for cooperation. Following the practice of previous years, the Ideas Bank provides professional community development support for the UN Decade of Learning for Sustainability in cooperation with similar organisations from Nordic countries.

Community life and democracy

The significance for the rest of Europe and elsewhere of the adult training-based popular education practice in Scandinavia cannot be over-emphasised. It provides fertile soil for community development. Scandinavian popular education underpins democracy through communication, publicity, education and community involvement. Their study circle movements (based on small, informal groups), educational associations, popular universities, public libraries, folk high schools, national training committees, interest organisations, trade unions and extensive public funding are all part of this; all demonstrate the extent to which lifelong learning need not be just a slogan but can be made possible and accessible. Beginning with the campaigns of the Danish thinker N.F.S. Grundtvig and his followers in the 19th century, Scandinavian countries have made serious efforts in the area of popular education not only for people from disadvantaged backgrounds but for every member of society through their continuing education programmes. Arguably one of the secrets of the success of the Nordic welfare model has been the popular education system. It is not surprising that one of the EU's lifelong learning programmes is named after Grundtvig.

The Swedish foundation Centrum för Samhällsarbete och Mobilisering (CESAM) has promoted Swedish and European democracy through community development and community education:

> The goal of popular education ... is not exclusively passing over knowledge ... but also the communication of social experiences and the raising of awareness that can lead to a broader and more profound democracy. (CESAM, 1994, p 4)

CESAM was established in 1984 during a period of local government reform in Örebro. In the early period, CESAM's main objective was to bring decision making and public services closer to citizens, and to develop better cooperation between local authorities and the voluntary and community sector. Community development training courses were launched for government officials, and workshops and community study circles were organised for community activists. CESAM developed the idea of neighbourhood cooperatives, establishing a regional support centre for cooperatives. This has been replicated in every region of the country. More recently, CESAM has helped establish social management committees in a number of institutions such as schools and care centres. Members of these committees are recruited from the catchment area of a particular institution and are responsible for its entire management and budget. In cooperation with the University of Örebro, CESAM initiated the introduction of national 'democracy days', a three-day annual event bringing together decision makers, researchers and local project activists to investigate the state of democracy. Today, one of the main priorities of the organisation is to encourage national and European politicians to engage with civil society and promote processes of empowerment (Andersson, 2007).

Work undertaken by the Centres for Local Activity (CAL) in Poland is of interest because it does not take community development groups as a starting point but rather uses community development methods to change existing community institutions such as cultural centres, social support centres, schools and clubs into community development centres in areas where the local community is active. Training courses are used to encourage institutions to change. CAL's training organisation also undertakes vocational training.

One of the most recent Hungarian examples of community development learning is an agreement reached within the framework of a regional operational programme financed by the EU. The agreement has been signed by representatives of local authorities, entrepreneurs and civil society organisations for the period 2007–13. The programme's objective is for the region to take responsibility for its own development, to reduce the number of external initiatives and increase the number of internal ones. The programme has been coordinated by the Association of Community Workers in Upper-Kiskunság through a two-year development scheme involving facilitation and partnership training. The community development professionals employed on the scheme have done their best to involve all key actors in the programme and commit them to the development process. The participants involved decided that the main goal was to develop the human resources of the region and they have devised a strategy to implement this. The most important aspects of the strategy are:

• strengthening self-confidence and learning motivation;
• developing learning skills and capacities;
• enhancing local and regional community identity;
• developing confidence, social participation, cooperation, tolerance and solidarity both within and between the sectors;
• establishing local media;
• using a regional analysis and the major trends in development planning, the training strategy has focused on complementing existing forms of formal and informal adult training and education with new and up-to-date content;
• another important aspect is that of enhancing people's general and vocational knowledge and looking for opportunities to provide freely accessible adult education, both in the area of vocational courses and adult training courses generally.

Conclusion

Since the dawn of the Enlightenment at end of the 18th century, Europe has been developing a new system of socio-cultural education (Steele, 2007), encompassing folk high schools, settlement houses, scientific learning societies and local reading circles. At the same time, working class movements began developing trade union education and workers' associations. The history of adult education shows how these forms of organisation have changed over time. During the period of state socialism, it is likely that no other system changed more radically than the popular education and socio-cultural systems of the central and eastern European region. With the system of cultural centres, the state sought to centralise already established learning, adult training and popular education as well as civil manifestations of a society that had already moved towards modernisation. This system-like scheme of cultural centres built in all local communities was initially a direct way of implementing the cultural policy of the Stalinist dictatorship; it fulfilled an aggressive role of spreading ideology, serving as it did as an operational centre for totalitarian measures such as the establishment of compulsory membership of cooperatives that entailed the nationalisation of private property.

Thus it was not surprising that, when the dictatorship waned, there was little interest in cultural centres among the adult population. In the 1960s, cultural centres started to abandon their aggressive functions. In Hungary, this was as a result of the 1956 revolution. However, the new system could not respond to the challenges faced by the majority of the population in their daily lives and was therefore unable to assume a role in building communities and developing society. It was in the mid-1970s that Hungarian community development entered the process, starting to build interest in the cultural and training needs emerging from everyday situations and looking for ways to develop programmes based on social dialogue. The first community development workers started to motivate adult citizens for community learning and thus the organic link between community development and adult education began to develop.

The underlying theme of this chapter is that local communities and community groups have a major role to play in developing a collective existence. This, in turn, involves the acquisition, preservation and development of local culture and the reaffirmation of norms and values. If these are absent, social functionality and consumer culture will be wholly dominant and the gap between the institutions that run society and how they are experienced in everyday life will widen. When referring to a crisis of values, confidence and culture in central and eastern Europe, there is a need to recognise that without socialisation to community life and democracy the crisis will continue. The renewal of fragmented and atomised communities requires external intervention because most communities lack the resources to implement the renewal process. It is hoped that the examples given in this chapter clarify the need for community development interventions and justify the argument that community development should be supported to a greater extent in contributing to the socialisation process.

Popular education and adult training systems have been in a transformatory phase since the beginning of the democratic changes in central and eastern Europe. However, none of the newly formed political elites or governments has recognised the power that conscious and informed citizens, empowered by their own communities, can represent in a democracy. This, it is true, may reflect governments' sense of insecurity and a fear of releasing new human resources and energy that could not be controlled. If that is the case, it is a short-sighted position and one that, in the end, will do more harm than good. We are witnessing a rapid erosion of community-based systems, while the new social (mainly civil) systems are developing more slowly than previously expected. They also lack the necessary intellectual and physical infrastructure. The result is that the contribution of community development to socialisation is being marginalised.

FIVE

Economic wealth

Sunlight Development Trust

The Sunlight Centre is an award-winning community venue and social enterprise in north Gillingham, Kent, an area that comes within the 20 per cent most deprived wards in the UK. A former derelict laundry, the centre is a hive of activity run by a combination of professional staff and volunteers, most of whom live locally. Almost 90 per cent of the centre's running costs are funded by its social enterprise arm, which has an annual turnover of more than £200,000.

The centre has been successful with its fundraising from government, local authority and national lottery sources. It has been visited by senior politicians from the three main political parties and is seen as a showcase for local social enterprise and community empowerment. The fair trade café at the centre has enabled 70 people, in one year, to obtain experience and qualifications as catering trainees. Outreach work at local health centres has created 25 further job and training opportunities for local people.

It is the combination of social enterprise and a strong commitment to community involvement that is the secret of Sunlight's success. It also provides a consultancy service, offering advice to other enterprise initiatives. The proceeds from the service are put back into running the centre.

The above example suggests that various factors influence the successful operation of projects in the broad field of community economic development. These include:

• the scope of the project, especially when it forms part of a major regeneration scheme;
• the growing connections being made between community economic development and environmental issues; and
• the dependence of community economic development on community development.

This leads us to an appreciation of the importance, historically, of economic criteria for community development. In Chapter Three, we noted Britain's colonial administrators' use of community development. An important dimension of this was to encourage self-help among farmers in Africa and elsewhere. In the 1950s and 1960s, the United Nations (UN) produced papers and guidelines on community development with the aim of encouraging member states to use community development as a key component of their development planning. In some countries, departments of community development were set up and continued after independence. From the 1960s onwards, in both the US and the UK, the economic dimension of community development became increasingly apparent, initially in the former's War on Poverty initiative and the latter's Community Development Projects and then in the major urban regeneration programmes launched in both countries in the 1980s and 1990s. Since then, the links between economic and community development have become increasingly evident. Sometimes, indeed, government and European Union (EU) statements and documents make it seem as if the entire rationale for community development rests on its potential for increasing economic wealth. At the same time, in southern countries, non-governmental organisations (NGOs) and community groups attach great importance to the connections between economic and community development in numerous ways, notably through women's cooperatives.

The alliance between economic and community development has not, of course, been a straightforward progression. In Scotland, for example, local authorities lost their enthusiasm for supporting community businesses, and in southern countries some governments have taken repressive action against NGOs and civil society, resulting in the decline of initiatives. There is also evidence that community development principles and practice can be weakened in situations where there are demanding requirements for economic outputs. The tension between, on the one hand, recognising the significance of economic factors for communities and their future and, on the other, assuming that economic criteria are the sole consideration for community development will be a recurring theme in this chapter. Our intention is to convey the impressive scope of community economic development while also submitting this to critical analysis. The chapter includes discussion of UK government policies on community economic development and appraisal of different models that have emerged. We shall argue that the achievement of economic wealth for communities is only one dimension of community development.

Types of community economic development

The phrase 'community economic development' is deployed less than it was 20 years ago; in the UK context, the term 'social enterprise' is more often used as shorthand to refer to all community-based economic initiatives. Community economic development, however, provides a useful overarching framework that encompasses the following:

- *Community businesses:* these are community-based organisations that have social objectives. They are set up, mostly in disadvantaged areas, to trade goods and services; any surpluses are reinvested in the business or the community. Businesses are controlled by local people and often run by them. The concept of a community business was popularised in Scotland in the 1970s and 1980s, but, following the decline of activity in that country, the term is now used rarely in the UK.
- *Social enterprise:* in addition to being used as the generic term for community economic development, social enterprise has also replaced the term 'community business'. It now reaches out to a broader constituency – see the membership of the Social Enterprise Coalition (www.socialenterprise.org.uk). The commitment to social and environmental goals remains, but much more attention is given to the central role of individual leaders. Examples of social enterprise in the UK are the setting up and running of *The Big Issue* (a magazine sold on the streets by homeless people) and the London restaurant Fifteen, an initiative of celebrity chef Jamie Oliver that provides training for disadvantaged young people. There are more than 60,000 social enterprises in the UK contributing nearly £10 billion to the economy. They are sometimes referred to as the business model of the 21st century. The arrival of social enterprise in the voluntary and community sector has resulted in a market-led approach being taken to meeting needs.
- *Development trusts:* these are organisations that trade for social purposes and manage the ownership of buildings and land (assets) to bring about long-term social, economic and environmental benefits in communities. Development trusts are independent, not-for-profit organisations that aim to be self-sufficient. There are 444 of them in the UK (www.dta.org.uk).
- *Asset-based community development:* this is a relatively new approach to community development and is put forward by its advocates as an alternative to what they see as the problem-focused approach of most community development. Asset-based community

development argues that community development occurs when people understand the potential of all their local assets. Supporters of asset-based community development go out of their way to insist that 'assets' covers a broad range – physical, cultural, social and spiritual. The main thrust of the approach, however, is on physical assets and their potential for generating income.

- *Cooperatives:* there is a long and impressive history of community cooperatives in Europe. Over the past 50 years, housing cooperatives have become an increasingly important part of the social economy, ranging from large city-centre blocks of flats to small rural cooperatives. In recent years the number of food cooperatives set up in the UK has increased significantly. Central to the definition of a cooperative is member ownership. Equally important, however, in the community development context is the commitment to contributing to community benefit.

- *Credit unions:* these started in Germany 150 years ago and have spread throughout Europe and to the US, Canada and Asia. One third of adults in Ireland are members of a credit union. Credit unions provide opportunities for savings and low interest loans to members. They are strongly community-based, democratically run cooperatives that often provide a focal point for community action. They are cheap to run and money is kept in the community. In poor neighbourhoods they provide an accessible alternative to the demands of 'loan sharks'.

- *Local exchange trading schemes (LETS):* these are mutual aid networks within which goods and services are exchanged without the need for money. A system of community credits is used: people earn credits by providing a service and can then spend these credits on whatever is offered by others in the scheme. LETS are run democratically, often as cooperatives. Time banks, through which people build up hours through services they provide, are a variation on LETS. One hour of a person's time entitles them to an hour of someone else's time.

- *Banking plays a key part in community economic development:* In the US, the 1977 Community Reinvestment Act (CRA) has resulted in commercial banks making loans to community groups in poor areas that wish to launch enterprise initiatives. (The sub-prime crisis of 2004–07 has resulted in a controversy on the extent to which the CRA was responsible for fuelling the crisis.) In Bangladesh, the Grameen Bank has achieved astonishing results with its policy of lending credits without any collateral. Nearly all the borrowers are women. The loan recovery rate is 98 per cent.

Central and eastern Europe

One of the major challenges facing central and eastern Europe since the regime changes has been how to enable local communities to contribute to the growth and development of their living standards. The 'socialist' economy did not demand this contribution, although from the late 1970s the Hungarian state party did allow people to benefit from the so-called second economy, which was a limited form of private economy. Small-scale agricultural production provided the broadest framework for this second economy, built largely on earlier community and economic traditions. It also, however, gained considerable influence in small-scale industries and trades, as well as white-collar professions. The second economy was built on the first economy and would not have been viable without it. Since the socialist economy was a deficit-producing economy, these modest, capital-lacking small enterprises were suitable for supplementing the incomes of families and individuals. However, in the fight for individual wellbeing, communities were sidelined.

Annual surveys undertaken by the Hungarian Association for Community Development (HACD) since 2004 indicate that today the situation is essentially the same, at least from the community development perspective: participation levels and a sense of belonging to the community remain low. Although each community has its own local government, individual improvement is still considered more important than the welfare of the community as a whole. This mentality changes slowly. Scarcely any investment has been made in Hungarian society and community development since 1989. This is astonishing given that the two principal conditions for community renewal are the power of belonging to the community and a high level of participation. Community development engages with the economic needs of communities because it is capable of strengthening a sense of belonging. It enhances the involvement of residents in their own affairs, including economic-related community activities. In this sense, economic and community development exist in symbiosis.

In cultures such as that of Romany people, community development has been shown to be extremely difficult, even with professional help from outside (see Schuringa, 2005). In Bulgaria and Hungary, for example, there have been a small number of community development initiatives aimed at improving the Romany minority's living standards but they have had limited success. The experiences indicate that the participation of the Roma can be enhanced for the interest of the individual and the family but not yet for the sake of the minority group or the local community as a whole. Even support for the individual and family can only be effective if the intervention goes beyond taking the initiative and provides professional assistance to include the granting of credit and long-term involvement in managing a business.

Case studies

The following case studies illustrate some of the challenges facing community economic development in the region.

Supporting income generation initiatives in Bulgaria

Creating Effective Grassroots Alternatives Foundation (CEGA) works for sustainable democratic development in Bulgaria by stimulating citizens' involvement at community level. Its long-term priority is to provide equal access to development for isolated and marginalised communities and groups. CEGA is one of the few NGOs in Bulgaria that are developing programmes to support low-income groups in ways that are consistent with the requirements of a market economy at the same time as providing development opportunities for marginalised groups. This has been achieved by supporting two main types of activity: agricultural initiatives (assisting landless Roma families to achieve economic independence through sustainable farming) and non-agricultural income generation projects.

The agricultural programme started in 1997. During the three-year pilot phase, it became clear that providing only financial support or training was not enough to help the participating Roma families to become good agricultural producers. The key was to combine access to information with formal training and financial support and to target not the individual but the family.

The Agro-Information Centre was established in Plovdiv in 2000. Its main task is to organise the development of human capital. The Land Limited Liability Company is a legal structure that manages a regional revolving fund. In 2003 CEGA finalised the strategy for decentralisation of the programme. The management was transferred to the newly registered Land – Source of Income Foundation that manages the Agro-Information Centre (Grigorova and Georgiev, 2008).

The Autonomy Foundation

The Autonomy Foundation (AF) has been active in Hungary since 1990, working mainly with Roma organisations. It was the first organisation in the country to test the method of providing credit to groups. Since 2004 this activity has been undertaken through the Mikrocredit share company, established with funding from the Soros Foundation. The reason behind this was that credit activities come within the scope of the Banking Act (1996) and can only be performed by business organisations under strict rules and supervision.

AF offers three kinds of credit: non-profit credit for civil organisations to help them cope with liquidity problems, collective credit, and micro-credit for small enterprises. Collective credit is provided to groups of people who are perceived by commercial banks to lack credit-worthiness; they do not have appropriate security or administrative capacity and are looking for small amounts of money for flexible short-term credit.

People joining a group take responsibility for each other. AF applies a method that has spread throughout eastern Europe: formal security is not requested but there is a contract of collective responsibility. AF formalises who will stand security for whom, and with what amount. AF launched the programme in four counties and has worked with 23 groups and 154 individuals. The maximum credit given out has been £310,000 for a 12-month period. Collective credits have been given to groups dealing with stock breeding and most credits have gone to groups involved with farming.

In this way, previously non-existent services have been created in many communities. A total of £2 million has been credited and a little more than half of it has been repaid. The 'lost' money can be explained in several ways. For example, the crediting process may not have been planned well or it may be difficult to bring together groups each of which is focused on achieving specific goals. There is also a serious shortage of formal entrepreneurial experience (there is only informal experience from the 'black' or 'grey' economy). Many people changed the credit into consumer credit as soon as a problem arose, trying to minimise loss ('If I don't pay the instalments, I will lose less'). Another reason for the failure could have been the difficulty of planning social transfers (constantly changing social provisions). Instalments were not always paid from people's entrepreneurial income but from social benefits.

The project failed to convey to participants the idea that the kind of credit promoted by AF is essential for them to make some kind of progress. Belonging to a group has the advantage of providing a profile. As a result, efforts to give collective crediting a symbolic significance in Hungary appear to have failed.

This was a pilot project, the analysis of which led to the conclusion that the Hungarian socioeconomic features related to this type of credit differ greatly from those of developing countries. This is neither a failure nor a success story, but a learning process. Sufficient experience has been accumulated and the programme

> is now being revised using the results of market research so that credit can be provided in an efficient and sustainable way (Béres, 2008).

Hungarian community development professionals have been involved with cooperative development since 1992. Only a small number of cooperatives, however, have been established since then, chiefly because the legal requirements make the setting up of cooperatives a difficult and expensive task. A new cooperative law of 2006 provides more favourable conditions for this form of community economic development. In 2007 the largest national organisation supporting employment, the National Employment Foundation, announced grant programmes for training mentors to support social cooperatives and help establish new ones. Below is a summary of one of the most promising proposals. It regards cooperatives not only as a means of making a living but also as a community enterprise. This also promotes the development of the area.

Community TV

In a small region consisting of 10 communities in central Hungary, young people established a social cooperative for the promotion of communication between communities. The regional union of local authorities raised funds for developing cable TV, broadband internet and a telephone network for the area.

The union called on the Association of Community Workers in Upper-Kiskunság, which had been active in developing communities for almost 10 years, to help involve young people who were interested in making television programmes. As a result of the community development activities of the association, four students and three unemployed young people formed a team and attended training courses on organisational development, community media and the preparation of business plans. The participants also made study trips to different community television stations. The training courses were conducted by professional community development workers.

The young people chose the social cooperative as an organisational form because they conceive of their work as being in the community and for the community. In the newly formed cooperative they can provide jobs for three young people and work experience for another 10 professionals starting their careers. In relation to the future of the area and retaining its population, they consider it crucial that people have access to as much information on their community as possible and are able to build contact with each other, for example, in the course of interactive computer programmes. With the help of Community TV, residents have a chance to get to know each other better so that regional identity and community networking are strengthened.

The young people targeted not only the development of their region but also people of their own age. Building on their initiative, they are willing to engage with young people, involving them in further community programmes (Hunti and Halmai, 2008).

Types of community economic development are not always distinct from each other. There are overlaps between them and in some projects two or more types can exist alongside each other. The examples, however, convey the essential elements contained in schemes that are aimed at strengthening the economic wealth of communities. These can be identified as follows:

- bringing economic benefits to individuals, families and groups through trading;
- a focus on local community needs and therefore a commitment, through a combination of paid staff and volunteers, to the provision of a variety of activities and services;
- reinvestment of any surplus into the project or enterprise;
- developing the skills and competences of local people to enable them to enter or re-enter the labour market.

The products and services that are provided through community economic development reflect the breadth of organisations and communities involved: housing cooperatives, shops and transport services, marketing of local crafts, tourism projects, managed workspaces, recycling and refurbishment projects, community arts festivals, printing and publishing, community cafés. These are just some of the activities that can be found in the sector. Increasingly, there are strong links being made with environmental issues and global justice.

Implications for community development

How do the economic criteria that are central to social enterprises and other types of community economic development relate to community development? What are the implications both for community development practice and communities themselves?

There can be no doubt of the extent to which economic considerations now influence community development. In some contexts these considerations have come to dominate decisions on community development strategies and practice. Indeed, in the minds of some senior managers, community development is assumed to equate with community economic development – the community development ideas put forward in this volume would be seen as dated and irrelevant to the imperatives that drive their programmes. This perspective is most evident in top-down regeneration programmes run by governments, the EU and other bodies in response to emerging problems in communities caused by economic globalisation and de-industrialisation.

A significant implication for community development of the dominance of economic criteria can be summarised by the term 'mainstreaming'. This means that community development, on the strength of its potential contribution to regeneration and economic development, becomes part of the government's central policy framework. This, arguably, is what has happened in both the UK and EU contexts. Gabriel Chanan and colleagues charted the trend in an analysis of UK regeneration programmes in the 1990s:

> With the change in orientation to community involvement in these national regeneration programmes – and a similar emphasis on the role of communities in many new unitary local authorities, and in the Social Exclusion Unit's strategy for neighbourhood renewal – community development is poised to move from its traditional 'experimental project' status to mainstream substance. This will require bolder strategies, higher skills levels and more thorough planning and management. (Chanan et al, 1999, p 4)

The trend towards mainstreaming continued during the next decade and so, too, did the preference of government to use the terms 'community involvement' and 'community engagement' rather than 'community development'. Chanan and colleagues refer to 'the new prominence of community involvement' and the change of language has been picked up by others. A working group set up by the Department for Communities and Local Government (DCLG) commented:

> The implementation of policies on community involvement and engagement depends fundamentally on community development. Yet community development, which is a particular way of working with communities, has an unclear

profile, and policy-makers and public alike are not yet fully aware of its crucial role in society. (DCLG, 2006a, p 3)

The changing language surrounding community development is more than simply a linguistic discussion and we return to this later. Here we need to acknowledge the dilemma posed by the mainstreaming of community development within an essentially economic policy framework, at least within the UK context. For a long time those people working within community development were aware of the extent to which they existed on the margins of policymaking, believing that this placed them in a fundamentally weak position; they could not monitor the ideas and strategies being formulated by powerful local and national agencies, nor could they advocate in these arenas on behalf of communities. That was often one reason why some community development workers and sympathetic local elected members, local government officers and even civil servants argued the case for having community development managers, because the latter would be in a position to influence thinking and to work for change within organisational and policy systems. A number of local authorities adopted this strategy.

Yet now that they are within the national policy framework – knocking on the door even if not sitting at the policy table – community development workers are concerned that their profession is in danger of being co-opted, brought within the system and thereby having its independence, its spark and capacity to challenge, threatened. This questioning of the position now occupied by community development is discussed by Michael Pitchford as a result of his interviews with experienced community development workers who were asked to compare practice today with practice in the 1970s and 1980s:

> Despite or because of the increasing incorporation of community development into government agendas, the community development field appears to have lost its way, with little direction or overarching purpose. Based on a process of social change for the benefit of communities, community development has moved away from what were felt by many to be 'idealistic' goals in the 1970s of reducing poverty and inequalities. These have been replaced by a more 'realistic' focus on involvement within participation structures to influence the quality and delivery of public services. (Pitchford, 2008, p 95)

This brings us to another implication for community development of the policy emphasis on economic criteria – the effects on communities. One aspect of this, the extent to which government insists on partnership working, has been extensively researched (see Balloch and Taylor, 2001, and Taylor, 2003). The evidence is that a combination of the procedures and demands of partnership working can all too often lead to the exhaustion of community representatives on partnership boards and, in worst-case scenarios, to the weakening of communities.

The more recent emphasis by government on empowerment does little to change the situation. The White Paper on community empowerment (DCLG, 2008) sets out how local people can be given more control over local decision making and yet there is little awareness of the effects such pressures can have on communities. It is as if the community development process and *conscientisation*, so fundamental to community development training and practice, have been put to one side. Empowerment is portrayed as almost a technical exercise in which communities are expected to participate. There is little sense of the struggles, frustrations and dilemmas that local people who become involved on behalf of their communities have to face. Nor is there an appreciation of the new perspectives and skills needed by public sector managers if the language of partnership working and empowerment is to have any meaning (see Butcher et al, 2007). However, it is the demands being made of communities that we highlight here. The emphasis on community enterprise and economic objectives combined with government advocacy of partnership and community empowerment is placing unrealistic and damaging demands on communities.

This connects with a further implication arising from the strong link between community enterprise and community development. It relates to the practice of community development as well as to the aspirations and resources of communities themselves. In particular, it highlights the position of community leaders. In the practice theory of community development that has evolved over the past 40 years, it is recognised that community leaders work on behalf of community groups. The latter are membership organisations, and leaders are accountable to them. Chairpersons of community groups are elected democratically for specified periods of time. Groups are entitled, indeed expected, to hold their leaders to account.

Social entrepreneurs

The emergence of community enterprise and the talking-up of the role of the social entrepreneur rest on a different premise. Social entrepreneurs represent a new breed of leadership. They are sceptical about the capacity of local authorities and other large welfare organisations to respond with sufficient flexibility and flair to social and economic problems. They do not assume that local people always know what they want; opportunities and choices need to be presented to them, accompanied where possible with costings and a business plan. According to Andrew Mawson, the founder of London's Bromley-by-Bow Centre, the key achievement of social entrepreneurs is to bring about connections. Social entrepreneurs are 'moving spirits' who seek new and innovatory solutions to social problems. They have touched a nerve that is familiar in community development: the failure of the traditional ways of delivering welfare state services, the need to cut through bureaucratic systems and reach out to ordinary people, a willingness to take risks. Social enterprise is nearly always a central part of any solution.

In this sense, social entrepreneurship is part of the tradition of innovation in British social policy. The School for Social Entrepreneurs was founded in 1997 by Michael Young, who, from his base at the Institute of Community Studies, launched many successful initiatives. There is little doubt that social entrepreneurship has made a mark. It is a product of our age; until the implosion of the western banking system in 2008, a belief in the cleverness and efficiency of the private sector worked in combination with a 'can do' philosophy. If, however, this aspect of community enterprise is analysed rigorously from a community development perspective, a number of questions can be raised:

- Is not the emphasis on the role of the individual leader, as well as the attributes or qualities said to be needed by the successful social entrepreneur, in tension with the core community development values of solidarity and collective action?
- Paradoxically, does not the approach of social entrepreneurship in making connections with a range of organisations and agencies feed into the government's partnership agenda, thereby potentially weakening the capacity of social entrepreneurs to question or challenge official policies?
- Is there a danger of the enterprise basis of social entrepreneurship distorting the nature of community needs, of formulating them always in economic terms?
- While community enterprises that use a social entrepreneurship model are committed to strengthening the voluntary and community sector and to building local resources that have one or more income

earning streams, how much of a priority do most social entrepreneurs attach to supporting grassroots social change? Do they challenge social and economic systems?

Asset-based community development

The approach of asset-based community development has a less obvious enterprise angle than social entrepreneurship. Implicit within it, however, is an economic framework. It is being used in a range of different contexts and with varying definitions. It is associated closely with the work of McKnight and Kretzmann in Chicago, deriving from their experience of the civil rights movement (Kretzmann and McKnight, 1993). In the UK, the approach has been taken up strongly by the Carnegie Commission for Rural Community Development:

> The vibrant rural community of the future will display an assets based approach rather than concentrating simply on needs, will use financial and other instruments to take ownership of community assets and will manage assets responsibly and actively over time for public benefit. (Carnegie Commission for Rural Community Development, 2007, p 20)

The interest being shown globally in asset-based community development is explained partly by the focus on participation and sustainable development – an asset-based approach can help governments and international agencies to legitimise their strategies. The Ford Foundation, for example, supports grantees in building assets that individuals, organisations and communities can acquire and develop. The assets include:

* financial holdings of low-income people, such as savings, home ownership and equity in business; and philanthropic capital such as permanent endowments built by and used for poor communities;
* natural resources such as forests, wildlife, land and livestock that can provide communities with sustainable livelihoods; these are often of cultural significance and provide environmental services such as a forest's role in cleansing, recycling and renewing air and water;
* social bonds and community relations – the social capital and civic culture of a place; these can break down the isolation of the poor, strengthen the relationships that provide security and support, and encourage community investment in institutions and individuals;

- human assets such as the marketable skills that allow low-income people to obtain and retain employment that pays living wages; and comprehensive reproductive health, which affects people's capacity to work, overcome poverty and lead satisfying lives (O'Leary, 2006, p 13).

In England, the Quirk review (DCLG, 2007) reinforces the government's desire to pass over more responsibility for public assets to communities:

> The fixed public assets in a community – the roads, the parks, the publicly owned land, buildings and facilities – are key resources for communities in their search for success but they are neither necessary nor sufficient conditions for their success. Confident, capable and ambitious community groups and social entrepreneurs can succeed on the flimsiest of asset bases and despite the apathy of established authority. (DCLG, 2007, p 4)

The main contention of those people who advocate asset-based community development is that it responds to the positive attributes of communities, in contrast to what they see as a needs-based approach of traditional community development:

> Asset based community development is an approach to working with communities that focuses on people's assets, rather than their deficiencies, and encourages the mobilising of community assets to meet opportunities for genuine community driven or citizen driven development. By focusing on 'the glass half full', it diverges from conventional development agency practice that focuses on problems and deficiencies. This shift is intended to correct the unintended outcome of well-intentioned community development efforts: communities that are inadvertently hobbled by a self-perception of inadequacy and a dependence on outside institutions for solutions to problems. (Mathie, 2006, p 2)

It is questionable whether this critique of so-called conventional practice is valid. One of community development's key characteristics has always been to seek out the strengths to be found in communities and to harness them in order that local people can respond actively to problems and needs. Assertions about the merits of asset-based community development require analysis. One problem is the language. To apply the term 'asset' so comprehensively to community development is strange. The word 'asset' originates from and belongs to the world of finance – investments, buildings, factories and other material things, most of which have the potential to generate profit. To extend the definition of 'asset' to include spiritual and other assets, however desirable, cannot pull the term away from its strong financial connotations. There is a clash, accordingly, with the language of community development, a language that is deeply embedded in human beings and human values.

In the past, community development has sometimes been guilty of exaggerating, even romanticising, the capacity of local people to bring about and handle change. Yet a belief in their resourcefulness and diversity is fundamental to community development. It can be released in many different ways, from organising social gatherings and festivals to running large-scale projects. The danger with the language of asset-based community development is its reductionism, narrowing down the interests of local people to developing and managing assets and thereby inevitably drawing them into an economic framework that in turn becomes the terms of reference for community development.

The last point alerts us to the risk that is run by an over-enthusiastic application of asset-based community development. Local people wish to be involved in decision making about local resources such as community centres, village halls and other amenities. They often also want a say in their governance. But do they necessarily want to own them and therefore have responsibility for their management and sustainability? The same people who are driven to initiate a project are not necessarily the same people who wish to maintain and service it: 'many residents who fight for a housing co-operative will not be as interested and effective in administering it' (Henderson and Thomas, 2002, p 219). If there is a strong, resourceful group behind a commitment to project management, this option is undoubtedly feasible. If, however, such a group does not exist, or if the implications of taking responsibility for an asset have not been fully worked through with local people, choosing such an option is questionable. Indeed, holding such a responsibility can become a trap for local people. Instead of being in the position of driving local development, they can all too easily become weighed down with the burdens of maintaining a building and, even more challenging, of ensuring that there is sufficient income to keep it going. In its report on seven rural and semi-rural trusts that have developed and managed community assets, the Development Trusts Association (DTA) records that one of them, Trinity Community Partnership, ceased trading during the course of the study. While noting that the problems it faced are a 'cautionary tale' for any trust that is endeavouring to develop an asset or deliver services under contract, it comments that:

> ... in some ways these problems have encouraged a new and innovative approach to delivering social good – through a new form of partnership involving the private sector and through entrepreneurship and enterprise. (DTA, 2008, p 44)

We see here both the confidence that drives the social enterprise movement and the presence of an assumption that social enterprise will always unlock problems. We question that assumption.

Community development has, on the whole, resisted being expected to take on the role of delivering services. Its purpose is to be a catalyst for bringing about change rather than be drawn into becoming one more part of the service delivery system provided by state, voluntary and private sector organisations. Yet the logic of asset-based community development leads communities directly down that path. It is this potentially powerful impact on the lives of local people that requires analysis. In the wider context there is also a question of the extent to which asset-based community development connects with social justice issues. This was the focus of a conference held in Glasgow in 2006, some speakers warning that, on its own, asset-based community development is not well placed to make the connections between local, national and international agendas:

> Like community development more generally, local solutions need to be linked to wider national, regional and international agendas for social justice, taking account of diversity and difference and inequalities within as well as between communities, and taking account of different approaches to representation and accountability. (Mayo, 2006, p 2)

Underlying theories

Four ideas that underpin community economic development have been evident in our appraisal: self-help, partnership, empowerment and capacity building.

The idea of *self-help* has a long pedigree in terms of both the individual (in the 19th century, Samual Smiles equated self-help with individual betterment) and the community (the colonial period of community development). Today the idea has acquired a connotation of enterprise, a 'get up and go' or 'can do' philosophy.

The term *partnership* in the community economic development context is more difficult to specify. Two core elements, however, can be identified: self-interest and efficiency. The former is to be found in organisational theory that explains why it is often in the interest of organisations to set up and be involved in coordination arrangements. These provide, for example, opportunities for an organisation to keep an eye on the plans and programmes of other organisations. Partnership working, accordingly, is a form of enlightened self-interest. It is also advocated, with good reason, as an efficient way of working because the resources of each organisation can be analysed and their deployment to best effect agreed.

As with the term 'community participation', *empowerment* is an idea that has obtained currency in such a variety of different contexts – including community development – that it can be understood only by examining the theoretical and ideological meanings behind it. This point is made by Hugh Butcher when setting out the concepts of power and empowerment as the foundation for critical community practice:

> Like most key concepts in the social sciences the concept of power is highly contested – that is to say its meaning will vary according to the 'paradigm' or theoretical 'frame of reference' in which it is embedded and used …. (Butcher, 2007, p 21)

Use of the idea of empowerment in the context of community economic development should be regarded cautiously. Compared with community development and community practice, its meaning in this context is underdeveloped.

The most significant underpinning theory for community economic development is to be found in the concept of *capacity building*. The term originated in North America and is widely used in the context of development programmes in southern countries. In her explanation of capacity building as an approach to development, Deborah Eade emphasises the importance of it keeping close to the development process:

> It is a response to the multi-dimensional processes of change, not a discrete or pre-packaged technical intervention intended to bring about a pre-defined outcome. In supporting organisations working for social justice, it is also

necessary to support the various capacities they require to
do this: intellectual, organisational, social, political, cultural,
material, practical or financial. (Eade, 1997, p 24)

When we explore how the concept of capacity building is used
in the US and the UK today we find that it has become coupled,
almost exclusively, with regeneration and economic development.
The European Commission used the term to underpin the strategies
it advocated for community economic development in areas of 'low
economic activity whose members have lost the ability to compete
in the labour market' (European Commission, 1996, p 85). More
recently capacity building has become the basis of many of the UK
government's policies. The UK Treasury has defined capacity building
as being concerned with building skills, knowledge, structures and
resources so that voluntary and community organisations can reach
their full potential in providing effective services (HM Treasury, 2002,
p 19). Thus capacity building retains its focus on training: 'activities,
resources and support that strengthen the skills, abilities and confidence
of people and community groups to take effective action and leading
roles in the development of communities' (Skinner, 2006, p 4). Even
among organisations that do not focus primarily on community
economic development, the tendency is to use the idea of capacity
building for that purpose:

> The impetus for capacity building in the faith sector arose
> from evidence that faith based organisations and faith
> communities were contributing, and could continue to
> contribute, to regeneration and civil and neighbourhood
> renewal. (Spratt and James, 2008, p 7)

Capacity building provides a helpful theoretical underpinning for
community economic development – a sense of direction and an
explanatory basis for economic initiatives. The danger, however, is
that it can come to be used simply in an instrumental or mechanistic
way (reflecting, perhaps, the term's use in engineering and other
industries). In their discussion of two approaches to capacity building
in the north-east of England – developmental and strategic – Sarah
Banks and Felicity Shenton point to the importance of being careful
to find out whether capacity building is what is wanted and needed
in an area and, if so, what will work:

> The instrumentality of some of the approaches that adopt
> the strategic approach to capacity building ... and the
> implication that capacity can be 'built' – rather like a bucket
> can be filled and its contents measured – signal caution not
> just in the use of the term, but also in its implementation. We
> need to question whose purpose capacity building is serving
> and ensure that local residents are not mere 'puppets' in the
> regeneration game played out by large national, regional and
> local agencies. (Banks and Shenton, 2001, p 297)

Conclusion

Our concern that capacity building can simply be an instrumental
element of regeneration programmes points to a broader conclusion
about economic wealth and community development. The economic
development dimension is of critical importance for communities'
quality of life. The downward spiral that can result from the closure of
a factory, coal mine or company in communities that have depended
on a single industry is known only too well. Local people become
demoralised, poverty increases, the built environment deteriorates,
existing and potential leaders leave the area, and inter-generational
conflicts and crime increase. The contribution of community
development in both preventing such situations from arising and
in responding to crises when they do arise has achieved widespread
recognition internationally.

Programmes that combine community and economic development
can produce significant results, bringing hope to communities and
providing the basis for making them stronger. They are, however, only
one part of the jigsaw. Economic wealth has to go alongside other key
components of a community's quality of life. This is explained clearly
in the framework for evaluating community development created by
Alan Barr and Stuart Hashagen. In addition to having an interest in
achieving shared wealth, local people can be concerned to create a
caring community, a safe and healthy community, a creative community
and a citizens' community. All of them encapsulate the idea of process
as well as outcome (Barr and Hashagen, 2000).

Our final comment on community economic development relates
to how community development programmes are planned and,
crucially, how community development is practised. If there is an
expectation that communities should take increased responsibility for
economic or enterprise activities, careful preparation with community
members is required before major decisions about funding, investment

and management are taken. If this is not done, experience suggests that there will be problems – even failures – and that the impact of this will fall predominantly on the community concerned. Equally, the community development profession needs to be clear that the criteria for evaluating the effectiveness of projects and programmes must go beyond the economic to include such critical elements of community development as community learning, informal networking and local leadership. Community economic development undertaken in tandem with community development has to be about a lot more than economic outcomes.

SIX

Social participation

> An important community function is that of providing local access to *social participation*.... Ordinarily, one thinks of voluntary organisations of various sorts as the community's most important units for channeling social participation. Nevertheless, many different types of social unit, including businesses, government offices, and voluntary and public health and welfare agencies, provide through their formal activity, important avenues of social participation to their employees or volunteer workers in the course of the performance of their occupational tasks. Likewise, family and kinship groups, friendship groups, and other less formal groupings provide important channels of social participation. (Warren, 1963, p 11, emphasis in original)

Debates about participation tend to focus either on users' involvement or on citizen participation and participatory democracy. Warren's concern with social participation across a range of 'social units' accordingly provides a useful counter-balance. It can also help us to unravel the meaning of participation in the context of community development. In a talk given at a conference of the Hungarian Association for Community Development (HACD), Vilnos Csányi pointed out that the social participation emphasised by Warren is a community function that facilitates the development of social organisations in which members of the community can become involved in establishing and shaping their community through community action. When this comes about, a loyalty towards the community emerges and this means that sometimes an individual will be ready to subordinate her or his interest to that of the community (Csányi, 2006).

This chapter begins with a discussion of the relationship between community development and social participation and the overall significance of participation. It also introduces the individual, community and political levels of participation. These levels can involve different types of participation that will be defined in relation to social and civil participation taken from social capital surveys. These forms of involvement can be used to highlight problems that involve change and renewal. We shall see that in central and eastern Europe, social participation is still much stronger than civil participation. Finally, we explore the issue of social inclusion in order to demonstrate how community development can contribute to the growth of participation and, therefore, to the strengthening of civil society.

Participation and community development

Community development aims to promote community involvement and social inclusion through participation. The overall goal is to strengthen the sense of belonging. For this to happen, people need to:

- be embedded in the community and society, not isolated from them;
- have opportunities to improve their living conditions; and
- be encouraged to engage in collective action that brings about positive changes.

A sense of belonging, however, is about more than an opportunity or a framework for action. It is also about human dignity. It means that, during the process of community development, community members are not treated as subjects but as partners; not as consumers but as human beings with an individual way of thinking; not as passive, indifferent, isolated residents but as active citizens; not as victims but as creators. They are people who:

- have contacts and relations with each other;
- cooperate with each other and help each other or accept help from others;
- deal with local issues and maintain dialogue with institutions and the outside world.

An individual who is rooted in a local community possesses a natural support network and contacts in which he or she both gives and receives, deciding who to give help to and who to receive help from without any assistance from outside. Community development promotes the joy of being able – and having the right – to give, recognising that the ability to give and the practice of giving develop the self-esteem and self-confidence not just of professionals but of all those involved. Belonging can be said to stand for participation itself. A member of a community group might say: 'I participate in the life of the community where I belong because I feel responsible for it and am ready to shape its relations, actions and objectives.'

Participation can be at both the individual and community level. With the former, participation means that individuals take control of their own lives; they take responsibility for themselves. Instead of drifting with events, they seek to control and create their own lives, formulating values, setting objectives and choosing people with whom to implement those objectives. At the community level, participation means people having contact with each other and the community, and the relationships this involves. It stands for people's confidence in each other, for mutual support and solidarity and for common norms and reciprocity. This, we shall see, is demonstrated by the concept of social capital.

Politically, participation is about the individual's involvement in the different levels of decision-making processes. This is how participatory democracy mostly manifests itself: participation enables the will of citizens to come across not through elected representatives but directly and this means that citizens and their organisations take part in the planning process that affects the community. The process starts with the assessment of needs, attitudes and demands, continues with the identification of areas for change and concludes with the elaboration and implementation of concrete plans. Planning is a cooperative process involving decisions at several points. Making a decision is an act of power, as it refers to the control of community resources.

Becoming involved in decision making requires a range of skills and capacities, such as being up to date and well informed; an understanding of a given issue in a wider context; familiarity with the capacities and resources of the community; and the ability to weigh up the possible effects of a decision. However, taking part in decision-making processes does not end with the act of making the decision. Controlling the implementation of decisions and being able to follow them up and make corrections is also necessary. Being involved in making decisions also requires a high level of civil awareness and an ability to exert influence over the long term.

People become involved in their communities in different ways, from a relatively low level of bonding, for example attending a local community meeting or club, to a high one, for example leading a campaign or being a representative on a community council. A high level of participation is a good indicator of a community that is working well. It is this, no doubt, that has resulted in participation having become so dominant within the thinking and practice not only of community development practitioners but also for a range of local, national and international policymakers. In a special issue of the *Community Development Journal* on participatory approaches in community development, Andrea Cornwall underlines the problematic nature of the topic:

> The widespread adoption of the language of participation across a spectrum of institutions, from radical NGOs to local government bodies to the World Bank, raises questions about what exactly this much-used buzzword has come to mean. An infinitely malleable concept, 'participation' can be used to evoke – and signify – almost anything that involves people. As such, it can easily be reframed to meet almost any demand made of it. (Cornwall, 2008, p 269)

Shelley Arnstein's ladder of participation (Arnstein, 1969) continues to be used in community development training because it demonstrates how easily participation can become tokenistic or manipulative and also because it points to the knowledge and skills required to bring about genuine participation. The increase in the number of tools and 'how to do it' guides to participation over the past 10 years has been in response to these challenges. Community development workers and other practitioners need to gauge levels of participation and the extent to which they are appropriate for particular situations.

Changing language

A critical analysis of the concept of participation is also needed because of the changing language of community development itself. This is especially apparent in the UK where the terms 'community involvement', 'community empowerment' and 'community engagement' have increasingly supplanted the term 'community development' in both policy and employment contexts. One commentator's explanation is to be found in the importance attached to community by the 1997–2010 Labour governments and their use of top-down policy solutions that have the effect of placing constraints on participation. It is the newer categories of 'community engagement' and 'community empowerment' rather than community development that, for example, underpinned the 2006 local government White Paper (Pitchford, 2008).

Engaging the public in the democratic process and encouraging people to take on some of the responsibilities traditionally held by local and national agencies are two reasons given for the change in language. In this way, community engagement and participation focus on communities and individuals helping themselves. Use of these terms is based on the premise of needing to promote personal responsibility and changes in behaviour on the part of deprived communities. It also seeks to involve community groups and individuals in service delivery.

The change of language matters for four reasons:

- It threatens to distort the essential purpose and goals of community development. Instead of being a springboard for transformation, community development is faced with the possibility of being harnessed to help implement the policies and programmes of national, regional and local organisations.
- Implicitly, it conveys a message that community development is by definition troublesome and uncooperative. In the UK context this is a message that has cast a shadow over community development since the Home Office Community Development Projects of 1968–76, which, using the practice and research of the projects, put forward a radical analysis of deprivation.
- It risks missing the point that, if they are to work, community engagement and community empowerment need to be underpinned by community development. On their own they can do very little – hence the recommendation in a Community Development Foundation booklet that 'all policies that invoke community empowerment or rely on community engagement should have a built-in margin of their budget allocated to community development and community capacity building' (Bowles, 2008, p 47).
- The new language fails to connect with theory – the ideas and explanations on which programmes and practice are based. Community development, in contrast, has a rich theoretical tradition. It is a tradition that sometimes lacks coherence and that contains ideological differences, but at least it exists. Theory is not a luxury. It provides an essential basis for practice.

Participation in the community development context raises a number of questions. The importance of being alert to the multiplicity of its potential uses is re-enforced by the changing language surrounding community development.

Community development and social capital

Trust and cooperation are the crucial elements of social capital. Making use of the concept in practice is challenging because, while one type of social capital brings those people who already know each other closer together, the other brings together people and groups who previously did not know each other. Alison Gilchrist, drawing on Woolcock (2001), summarises the different kinds of social capital:

- *bonding:* based on enduring, multi-faceted relationships between similar people with strong mutual commitments such as friends, family and other close-knit groups;
- *bridging:* formed from the connections between people who have less in common, but may have an overlapping interest, for example, between neighbours, colleagues or different groups within a community;
- *linking:* derived from the links between people or organisations beyond peer boundaries, cutting across status and similarity and enabling people to exert influence and reach resources outside their normal circles (Gilchrist, 2004, p 6).

The democratic deficit and lack of commonality are on the agenda of every European country. However, this set of problems presents itself in the new European democracies in a very direct way. Surveys that have focused on the measurement of social capital have provided HACD and its partner organisations with a framework for measuring the particular characteristics of civil society. Some of the community development-related questions raised by the surveys were selected and taken from the British Citizenship Survey conducted in 2001. The random sample appraisals in seven central and eastern European countries involved a total of 1,200 citizens from 13 local communities (three Bulgarian communities, three Ukrainian, two Czech, two Hungarian, one Romanian, one Russian and one Slovakian). The results provide clear evidence that the level of social participation in the region is much higher than that of citizen participation:

> While the highest level of activity in central and eastern European countries is to be found in groups, clubs and organisations, the situation is different when it comes to participation in civic affairs, an area of special importance for community development. (Vercseg, 2005, p 401)

Hungarian context

When comparing the structure of today's social capital with the social capital dominant before the democratic transformation, it is essential to recall the historical context and its continuing influence on people's attitudes and their willingness to take action in the public domain.

Following the softening of the Stalinist dictatorship in Hungary and other socialist countries, particular aspects of community life (mainly culture and leisure) were extended, generated largely by a well-organised network of cultural centres.

At the time of compulsory employment, every adult had to belong to an employment organisation. This secured a sense of belonging and built other forms of bonding outside the workplace, such as company day nurseries, preferential credit opportunities and collective savings banks in the area of social welfare; company cultural centres and sports centres in the spheres of education, culture and leisure; and dances, brigade meetings, excursions and company holidays in the area of social gatherings. In the period of state socialism during the 1980s, socialist companies often sponsored community events and development schemes. Naturally, these forms of benefit and support could be very different in a city-based company than in a village cooperative or industrial workshop, but in one form or another they existed everywhere.

It is not entirely fair, therefore, to blame the power of the state for the lack of community. What we saw then was that people were not concerned with issues of their locality. We found that the local community was only a place for existing in, a neighbourhood where residents worked to improve their own homes and strove exclusively for their own prosperity. Paradoxically, the so-called 'bee work', a form of collective help, still existed in those times; when building a house or performing larger-scale agricultural activities, or even just repairing a car, neighbours and relatives used to help each other out on a reciprocal basis. Unfortunately, this practice has since been lost, due partly to the fact that it is often regarded by the authorities as being part of the informal economy.

Although the existence of a kind of communality during the time of the state party system has come to be recognised, the social experiences obtained later make it clear that the socialist regime did not favour action at the local level. It had good reason for this. In a centralised, hierarchical and closed social structure, such things as locality, local communities or their smaller neighbourhood units could not even be talked about. Locality was rediscovered at the beginning of the 1980s by empirical and sociological work dealing with local society and local power, and by the first experiments in local community development that sought to look at local society as a whole. This rediscovery concerned the complexity of locality: the identity and communality – or the lack of them – that relate to power structures, the economy, people's mentality and awareness, their spirituality and history. This early community development discovered that a society that is atomised, unstructured, unorganised and unwilling to cooperate is defenceless against state power and can be kept in a position of dependency (Varga and Vercseg, 1998).

In the light of today's shortcomings, there is an appreciation that, prior to the post-1989 changes, the different disciplines, work organisations and educational institutions of a particular region used to maintain contact with each other. Today, we would say that they engaged in networking and in organising joint events. People doing similar jobs used to know each other and communicate regularly. There was, therefore, an element of commonality, namely social participation, that was surprisingly strong in central and eastern Europe at that time. Collective action also had a chance to unfold in such areas as culture, leisure, sports and amateur arts, and in the different age-related movements such as youth clubs and the pensioner movement. The effects of this latter phenomenon are still evident today. Of the population engaged with community development, it is still people aged 50-70 who are usually mobilised first among the different age groups. These people were socialised during the years of 'socialism', when they had a chance to acquire the skills of collective action and organisation at the leader training courses of different movements. Paradoxically, therefore, under the aegis of 'democratic socialism', these people also learnt a lot about democracy. This should still be considered of value today, even though during the earlier period people did not have a chance to transfer their knowledge into action. But the knowledge and practice became part of the culture of this generation and forms an important element of the social capital brought from the past. It is still at work today.

The same did not hold true, however, for public and political involvement, self-organisation and citizen participation. Despite the gradual modernisation of the central and eastern European region during the one-party system, active involvement in public life and public affairs could not gain ground. In an era of centralised decision-making mechanisms and redistribution, it would have endangered the very foundations of the system. The logic of the state system simply could not permit the emergence of citizen participation. We can highlight this from research in a very different context:

> The very concept of citizenship is stunted there.... From the point of view of inhabitants, public affairs is somebody else's business – *i notabi*, 'the bosses', 'the politicians' – but not theirs. Laws, almost everyone agrees, are made to be

broken, but fearing others' lawlessness, everyone demands sterner discipline. Trapped in these interlocking vicious circles, nearly everyone feels powerless, exploited, and unhappy. (Putnam, 1993, p 29)

In this study of 'uncivil' regions in Italy, Putnam could have been describing central and eastern Europe in the 1980s!

Our conclusion is that the practice of today's most active generations in central and eastern Europe is relatively well developed in terms of social participation but weak in terms of citizen participation (Vercseg, 2004). It would be a mistake, however, to think that social participation is somehow less valuable than citizen participation. Our argument is that a certain level of social participation is a precondition for effective community development participation. When, however, citizen participation is considerably weaker than social participation, we can conclude that a democratic state is experiencing severe imbalances. It means that the scope for democratic processes is limited and that institutions become inward-looking and defensive. It is why the struggle to strengthen civil society is so central for a well-functioning and vibrant democracy.

Regardless of which type of participation we examine, the extent to which young people are inactive is striking. What kind of social capital will we be able to talk about when the older generations give way to the younger ones? Will it be that social capital will be regarded as a private good?

Social capital can be exhausted and become outdated. Furthermore, the balance between its social and private sector dimensions can change, as can the extent to which it is spontaneous or the result of professional intervention. Evidence that the concept of social capital is gaining ground globally suggests that in post-modern societies the decline and, in varying degrees, the lack of social capital is becoming increasingly recognised. This may be especially true for post-communist countries but it is also increasingly apparent in western societies whose economic and social assumptions have been challenged as a consequence of the 2008–09 financial crisis. Putnam argues that we must weigh up the risks of destroying social capital:

> Precisely because social capital is a public good, the costs of closing factories and destroying communities go beyond the personal trauma borne by individuals. Worse yet, some government programs themselves, such as urban renewal and public housing projects, have heedlessly ravaged existing

> social networks. The fact that these collective costs are not well measured by our current accounting schemes does not mean that they are not real. Shred enough of the social fabric and we all pay. (Putnam, 1993, p 34)

It is often said that the culture of democracy needs considerable time to become established. However, by involving what are known as 'accelerator institutions', this process can take place at a much quicker pace and in a less painful way, with no further collective losses occurring. Community development is one such accelerator institution, as are education, adult training and learning for a new culture. This means that community development has extraordinary potential to bring about change and to re-invigorate the social capital of disadvantaged communities. The emphasis of social capital theory on trust and cooperation connects strongly with community development principles and practice. It is essential in community development to have a baseline of trust among people and a willingness to cooperate – hence the investment of time and skills by community development workers in building such a baseline. The following case study illustrates the process through which a community that seeks to take action will go.

Community development in Tordas

In 2007, an investment company planned to open a brick factory and clay mine in Tordas, a village of 1,800 inhabitants in western Hungary. According to the local authorities, this would have created jobs and a considerable tax income for the impoverished village. However, local community groups had a different opinion. They were convinced that mining would involve a lot of dust and noise, and that smoke from the brick factory would affect the health of local people. After endless debates, the authorities announced a referendum to decide on the issue, while local community groups organised a forum for their members and started to investigate the possible advantages and disadvantages of the project. They organised study visits to other communities that already had a brick factory, and they invited and consulted a wide range of experts and professionals. Both the local authorities and the community groups issued information leaflets that were delivered to all homes. Seventy-seven per cent of the residents voted in the referendum. The 'no' answers outnumbered the 'yes' answers by two to one – local people rejected the investment.

Local community groups demanded help from community development workers and started to work on improving the financial situation of the local council. Their goal was to avoid having those who voted against the planned factory think that they had 'defeated' the local council, thereby allowing the local authority to strike back by saying that the lack of funds was due to the fact that local people hindered development. Soon they recognised the urgent need for collective reflection and cooperation. They conducted a community appraisal of the development prospects of the local community. This was followed by a well-organised consultation process between members of community groups and local elected representatives. Through this active dialogue, the proposals and ideas of local residents have been considered with the objective of developing a long-term local development plan and vision for the community. A citizens' council has been set up, preceded by an informal training course organised by community development workers. The citizens' council has submitted its proposals to the board of local elected representatives.

This example shows that spontaneous community action can sometimes risk ending in 'lose–lose' situations that may require searching for a way forward. It is also possible to build up a community structure that, through ensuring a high level of participation, can facilitate the development of the community and result in 'win–win' situations.

The main issue facing central and eastern European countries is the extent to which societies are prepared to make sacrifices in order to regenerate the injured tissues of commonality and civil society, to develop capacities and functions that have not even begun to be elaborated and to strengthen social and civil participation. These goals are captured by the phrase 'the renewal of social capital', reproducing it in an expanded way and in a more up-to-date structure.

Social inclusion

The concept of social inclusion fits closely with community development values and principles. It also conveys many of the issues and goals referred to above. Social inclusion is about enabling everyone to take an active part in society. Community development workers have a key role to play in enabling the processes that lead to inclusion to take place. Participation, however, can also be achieved on its own, without help from professionals. The time and extent of a possible intervention from outside depends on the community's level of education, organisation, civil culture and discipline. Usually we talk about the need for social inclusion when local people show a low level of participatory activity in the interactions and institutional processes of the community and society. This is demonstrated when confidence towards each other and solidarity are weak, mutual help and the extent of active relationships are low and residents are unfamiliar with their rights, obligations and opportunities. At the same time, local institutions, while in theory working on behalf of local people, do little to encourage community involvement. Only a small number of people are engaged in decision-making processes.

In western Europe, the need for social inclusion is advocated with reference to socially excluded groups and communities. In 2010, the Year for Combating Poverty and Social Exclusion, the European Anti-Poverty Network aims to show the enriching impact of the participation of people experiencing poverty. It is aware, however, of how this issue has to be handled carefully. The same is true of community development; many people do not want to be labelled as poor or excluded, sometimes local people will disagree strongly with each other and, finally, those who are marginalised in society will frequently be criticised by others. These feelings have to be dealt with by anti-poverty and community development workers.

In the case of the new democracies, the non-democratic historical experiences accumulated over the centuries have had a decisive effect on the need for extending social inclusion. In this way, the sharing of responsibility and participation, which used to be exclusively owned by the state and its institutions, affects almost the entire populations of these countries.

The moral argument for favouring participation and social inclusion is only part of the picture. Increasingly, it is economic considerations that drive the promotion of participation and inclusion, as we saw in the previous chapter. The crisis of the welfare system, the recognition of the need to shift from government to governance and the involvement of citizens and their organisations in a wide range of social services are perceived as reducing the demands for support needed by citizens and communities. They become equipped to organise their own lives, with a decreasing level of support from the outside. Thus self-help is realised in many different ways. Activity replaces passivity.

All this assumes the existence of an alert community development profession. Community development workers must always question the actions of policymakers and managers. They must only promote processes that comply with community development principles, above all those of equality and solidarity, collectivity and respect, citizen action and the service of the common good. Community development should only support processes that do not hinder the emergence of community action and that allow for freedom and independence and the presence of a critical attitude. Indeed, it should seek to strengthen these processes in multiple ways.

Conclusion

The importance of social participation as a building block for community development needs greater recognition. On occasions, it seems as if community development is being swept along in the wider context as part of the search for ways of engaging citizens and strengthening democracy. What is it, however, that enables people to join in these debates? What moves people to work together in groups and organisations? Running through this chapter is the argument that trust between people has to be allowed to grow, especially if there have been conflicts in the past. The same argument applies to the regeneration programmes that have played such a dominant part in western European communities over the past 20 years. Too often there has been an assumption by the managers of these programmes that local people will simply respond to proposals put to them and be prepared to accept the constraints that nearly always form part of such programmes. This, in our experience, reflects a superficial understanding of participation because it does not take sufficiently seriously the process that is required to enable people to participate. It also places too many conditions on people's participation, discouraging them from questioning the options that are put forward and opposing any wishes they may have in challenging the options and presenting alternatives.

Community development workers should always ask the question, what lies behind participation schemes and models? What makes them work? How are failed schemes explained? These questions can be asked of large schemes, such as the local participatory budgeting developed originally in Porto Alegre, Brazil, and of small, neighbourhood-based partnership schemes that extol the value of participation. They can also be asked about people's participation in the techniques and models that have been developed by planners and others to facilitate participation – Planning for Real, village appraisals and future workshops, for example. These techniques can be used very effectively to help people have a say in the futures of their communities and they have been developed in response to people's demands to be listened to. They must, however, be more than short-term, ephemeral episodes in a community's life. They need to be based on the realities of how people relate to each other – or fail to do so. Explanations for successful and failed participation schemes may be found in people's memories about their neighbours and in deeply engrained hopes and fears about their community. This is where community development has a crucially important role to play because it has theoretical knowledge and practice experience of

—

how communities reach the point of being willing to organise and take action.

Central to the recognition of the place of social participation in community development is the existence of a strategy, whether one is talking about an intervention in one community by one worker or fine-tuning the approach to be taken by an organisation that has committed itself to using community development. Setting out a strategy forces those involved to specify the goals and objectives of an intervention and the methods that will be used. In that way, time and space can be obtained for working on social participation. It ceases to be a vague good intention and instead becomes an essential and defined part of community development. There is an irony in the need for community development to adopt a strategic approach when, in reality, the actual practice is usually full of turmoil, false starts, victories and confusion. It is an irony, however, that should be celebrated because it underlines the particular characteristics of community development as well as its potential for bringing about positive change.

SEVEN

Social control

Arguably the most visible presence of social control in the community is 'neighbourhood watch'. Often referred to as the 'eyes and ears' of the police, neighbourhood watch schemes are to be found in urban and rural communities, most notably in the UK and the US. Their purpose is to alert the police to incidents that appear to be breaking the law and to report suspicious or threatening behaviour by strangers. Schemes announce their presence with signs stating 'This is a neighbourhood watch area'. Some of them exist in name only; others are well organised and active. There is evidence to suggest that the latter tend to be more prevalent in middle-class communities.

The issue of social control is almost always a high priority for communities – both those that experience acute forms of deprivation and so-called 'gated' communities where the homes of the well-off are protected by walls and fences in order to eliminate contact with the wider community. Fear of crime is dominant within our psyches and it is fuelled by the separation between social classes, between the well-off and the poor. Inevitably, it is heightened in communities where there are significant numbers of young people and where the crime rate is perceived to be high. Politicians are aware of the potency of social control and do not hesitate to introduce new policies and legislation in order to demonstrate their capacity to respond to the anxieties and fears of local people. As a consequence:

> Evidence-based research and policy is made on the basis of what is most likely to please a public misinformed by a media which is actively fuelling the culture of fear. (Minton, 2008, p 7)

Social control assumes the presence of mechanisms and sanctions that regulate the behaviour of individuals and groups in order that people can live in a society that conforms to certain values and norms. All of us are concerned about social control – how to feel and be safe within society. The key question is how to handle the concern, how to achieve the right balance between the various means available to create and maintain social control. These include measures such as curfews to restrict people's movements, forms of punishment in the community, high levels of surveillance (CCTV, policing) and community involvement, whether through neighbourhood watch or other schemes.

In this chapter, we shall argue that community development can contribute significantly to social control but that, in most instances, attempts to involve local people in social control have used a misleading or restricted understanding of community development. This has resulted in a weakening of the effectiveness of community development with regard to social control. When compared with community development's contribution in other spheres – housing and economic development, for example – its contribution to social control has been minimal. The chapter begins with a discussion of community development and social control in the UK context. We then put forward a model that we believe can form the basis of a community development approach to social control. In a final section, we present a Hungarian perspective on social control and community development.

Punishment and community

In November 2008, the World Health Organization's Regional Office for Europe organised a conference in Kiev on women's health in prison. It resulted in a Declaration that sought to raise awareness across Europe of the current situation regarding the health of women in prisons and the healthcare provided. The Declaration called for improvements by implementation of recommendations for:

- a more acceptable and gender-sensitive criminal justice system with special attention to the rights of women and children;
- prison healthcare that is at least broadly equivalent, in terms of amount and quality, to the healthcare provided in the community; and
- satisfactory methods for ensuring continuity of care.

This example is about a minority; women make up only a very small proportion of the UK prison population. Most prisoners are men aged 16–18. In recent years, however, there has been growing concern about women in prison, because of both high suicide and attempted suicide rates and the high social costs of incarceration for women and children.

The example draws attention to the lack of resources available for good-quality, non-custodial schemes, notably restorative justice. The Declaration demonstrates the connections between prison and community and highlights the importance of investing in prevention

—

– to reduce opportunities for offending taking place. As the authors of the article on the Declaration comment:

> There is a need for an integrated approach to women's offending. Many women could be kept out of prison if the causes of their offending behaviour were addressed in the community before they commit the crimes which lead to their imprisonment, causes such as poverty, abuse and violence against them and/or their children; and drug and alcohol addiction which are often caused by one or the other or both of the first two. (Scurfield, 2009, p 4)

Any discussion about prisons has to be placed in the wider context of inequality and social injustice. The number of prisoners goes up as the gulf between rich and poor people widens. This results in the building of more prisons and the incarceration of more people:

> In societies with greater inequality, where the social distances between people are greater, where attitudes of 'us and them' are more entrenched and where lack of trust and fear of crime are rife, public and policy makers alike are more willing to imprison people and adopt punitive attitudes towards the 'criminal elements' of society. More unequal societies are harsher, tougher places. (Wilkinson and Pickett, 2009, p 155)

It is the theme of prevention that provides a powerful underpinning for strengthening the case for investing in community development approaches to social control. The problem is that all too often these approaches are pushed to one side by populist notions of punishment and community. We have the example of the scheme that requires those people doing community service to wear a 'community payback' high-visibility jacket, thereby drawing attention to the fact that they are offenders. The previous UK government also had plans to give the public a greater say in the handling of low-level crimes such as disorderly conduct, possibly through local votes on punishments such as clearing graffiti. It had extended the community courts schemes begun in Liverpool and Salford to 10 other areas. Such schemes involve judges and magistrates interacting with local people in places such as community centres and closely following the progress of individual offenders. The argument for taking forward these kinds of scheme is that, by involving communities in decisions about the work that offenders should undertake in the community and by seeing them do it, the confidence of communities in engaging with issues of social control is built. Is it, however, the most effective way of strengthening communities and is there not a danger that visible community punishment schemes will actually exacerbate enmity and suspicion between local people?

The tradition of having prison visitors and, until quite recently, the history of the probation and after care service in England and Wales testify to society's awareness of the importance of building links between prison and community. The probation service and the prison service are now integrated and form part of the National Offender Management Service (NOMS), based in the Ministry of Justice. NOMS has regional offices but continues to be run from the centre – a contrast to when the probation service was county-based with the capacity to make decisions according to area needs. More seriously, the role of probation has changed from being a reformist, social work agency engaged with the criminal justice system to being part of the law enforcement system. In the 1970s and early 1980s, there were many examples of probation teams engaging in community development. They managed to support community groups at the same time as they supervised offenders in the community (Henderson and del Tufo, 1991).

Today's political and social climate means that a change of heart from the Home Office and Ministry of Justice on the role of the probation service in community settings is very unlikely. Yet there remains a definite interest within government in community policing as well as a commitment to the police being members of partnerships in local areas. The White Paper *Building communities, beating crime* (Home Office, 2004) emphasised neighbourhood policing and this was re-enforced in the Flanagan report (Flanagan, 2008). There are more than 15,000 police community support officers employed throughout England and Wales. Their role is to act as a link between the public and uniformed officers particularly on matters relating to crime reduction and minor offences. The role is similar to that of neighbourhood wardens, who are employed by some local authorities.

Sometimes individual policemen and policewomen have taken active, lead roles in supporting community groups. This will come as a surprise to some people involved in community development who insist on assigning the police a traditional and restricted role aligned wholly with its law and order responsibilities. If opportunities for genuine community policing do exist, and if the case for expanding alternative, community-based schemes for offenders can be sustained, a community development approach to social control may indeed have the potential to be significant for the criminal justice system as well as for local organisations and communities.

Communities and social control

We move now to a very different angle on community development and social control. It assumes a broader definition of social control than that held by the framework of punishment, prisons and police that we have just discussed. It also takes seriously communities' fears and concerns about offending but argues that this on its own offers a limited understanding of social control in the community context. The fragmentation of social order, the existence or fear of violence and conflict, are of profound importance for communities and it is in response to such pressures that the scope for community involvement lies. The context in which this potential can be realised is threefold.

The breakdown of social institutions. A vibrant voluntary and community sector exists in many European countries. In addition to a wide range of voluntary organisations and community groups, the sector includes faith-based organisations and international non-governmental organisations (NGOs) .Yet in many communities the neighbourhood-based groups, organisations and networks that traditionally played a key role in maintaining social control have, in recent decades, been severely weakened.This is true most especially of communities that have experienced significant decline and that display the well-documented features of deprivation and social exclusion: unemployment, a deteriorating environment, extreme poverty and problems of conflict, violence, drugs misuse and offending. It is all too easy to fall into the trap of portraying communities of the past as being tight-knit, free of problems and supported by benevolent social institutions.This would be a travesty of the reality. On the other hand, there can be no doubt that many communities today have the feel of being deserts.They lack recognised structures and struggle to offer residents decent lives.

Security. CCTV forms part of our daily existence; Anna Minton describes Britain as 'the CCTV capital of the world, spending one fifth of the global total on the technology' (Minton, 2009, p 168). In shops, arcades and public spaces, cameras record people's movements – with considerable implications for police time spent analysing film. Proposals for personal information databases and identification cards could lead to increased levels of surveillance. Since the terrorist attacks of 11 September 2001 and 7 July 2005, governments have emphasised the need for increased security measures, leading to lively debates on security and civil liberties. In the context of communities, the UK government has introduced schemes aimed at countering the effects on local communities of the UK and the US governments' military involvement in Iraq and Afghanistan, as well as of events in Gaza. The Preventing Violent Extremism (PVE) programme is designed to minimise extremism and build the resilience and confidence of communities to counter the global terrorist ideology. Up to 70 local authority areas are thought to be susceptible to violent extremism. PVE initiatives include the teaching of citizenship in mosque schools and strengthening community leadership, focusing particularly on supporting those, including young people, who have links with the hardest-to-reach individuals. PVE has been criticised by some commentators chiefly because of concerns that the programme has a hidden agenda:

> Decisions are taken behind closed doors rather than in consultation with the voluntary and community sector. Rather than engaging local people democratically, many local authorities seem to take the view that decisions over Prevent are best made away from public scrutiny. (Kundnani, 2009, p 6)

The aim of building communities' confidence in the face of the security imperative connects with the other key policy of the UK government on the divisions and fragmentation in communities – community cohesion. This term was coined by Ted Cantle in his report on the race riots that took place in the northern towns of Bradford, Oldham and Burnley in 2001. The report found evidence of people living 'parallel lives' and it defined cohesion as being about building bridges between communities (Cantle, 2001). The potential contribution of community development in such complex and difficult processes is very evident. The community cohesion policy has been overshadowed by PVE and by the global politics surrounding it. A more robust commitment to using community development could help to make the idea of community cohesion more of a reality to people's lives. The government's action plan in response to the phenomenon of hate crimes – the targeting of individuals, groups and communities because of who they are – is an example of the scope for injecting a strong community development dimension. In his foreword to the action plan, the Home Secretary states:

> Hate crime is a human rights issue, a threat to community cohesion and a rejection of our shared values. Our society

is strong when communities are strong. And communities
thrive when they are united by positive values they share.
(HM Government, 2009, Foreword)

That, surely, points to the need for a community development input.

Fragility of representative democracy. As noted in Chapter Two, anxieties
among political scientists and others concerning low voter turnouts
at elections and a widespread disillusionment with the representative
political system have been expressed for a number of years. Reasons
for public disillusionment with conventional politics were put forward
by the Power Inquiry as follows:

- citizens do not feel that the processes of formal democracy
  offer them enough influence over political decisions –
  this includes party members who feel they have no say
  in policy-making and are increasingly disaffected;
- the main political parties are widely perceived to be too
  similar and lacking in principle;
- the electoral system is widely perceived as leading to
  unequal and wasted votes;
- political parties and elections require citizens to commit
  to too broad a range of policies;
- many people feel they lack information or knowledge
  about formal politics;
- voting procedures are regarded by some as inconvenient
  and unattractive. (Power Inquiry, 2006, pp 17–18)

Barack Obama's 2008 presidential campaign will be of historical
significance, as well as having contemporary relevance, because he
took these concerns seriously. The campaign used innovatory methods
that combined the use of new technology and, drawing on Obama's
experience as a community organiser, engaged in dialogue with
people on streets and doorsteps, demonstrating a willingness to listen
to opinions and to be informed about issues by local people.

One consequence of the uncertainties surrounding the future of
the representative political system and how it can exist alongside
a participatory system is to open up opportunities for far-right
movements and parties to capture people's attention. Members of
deprived communities are especially vulnerable, particularly in those
communities where Islamophobia is most virulent. The British National
Party (BNP) and other far-right parties now have this as their focus:

> Wherever we have explored tension between Muslims and
> the local community we tended to discover the BNP was
> present, fanning discontent. This should come as no surprise.
> All over Europe parties of the far-right have been dropping
> their hostility to minorities such as Jews and homosexuals
> and resorting instead to the politics of Islamophobia. The
> same trend is at work with Austria's Freedom Party and
> the French National Front. (Oborne and Jones, 2008, p 27)

The emergence of the BNP in English local politics is a warning
signal about the state of local democracy and has implications for how
communities under severe economic and social pressures can maintain
control of their environment. This is especially significant in areas
where local councils have few resources and feel relatively powerless
to address the underlying causes of xenophobia and neo-fascist local
politics (Wilks-Heeg, 2008). Where the conditions exist for far-right
activities, the issue of social control becomes inseparable from local,
national and international politics and the powerful changes that are
affecting communities.

How communities and organisations sought to maintain social control
within Republican/Nationalist and Loyalist communities – as well as
between them – during the 'Troubles' in Northern Ireland (1968–94)
tells us a great deal about what happens to social control in extreme
circumstances. Paramilitary organisations adopted alternative systems
of dealing with and controlling members of their own communities.
They operated outside the formal criminal justice system and used
warnings and punishments that included physical assaults, curfews,
fines, acts of public humiliation, intimidation, expulsions, property
damage and shootings. There was tribalism and vigilantism but also
inter-community policing where people and groups operated at the
interface between hostile communities.

Tensions that carry the danger of a breakdown of social control are
evident in the context of race and diversity issues in northern England.
The following extract is taken from a report prepared by Mike Waite, a
serving local government officer in Burnley, one of the towns dealing
with the aftermath of the 2001 disturbances:

> There is widespread recognition that the idea of
> 'multiculturalism' has become increasingly problematic.
> From the late 1960s onwards multiculturalism provided a
> conceptual framework for managing community relations
> in Britain, involving policies which recognised the distinct

identities of the different racial and cultural communities, and supported their diverse forms of life and organisation.... This framework has now come under severe pressure as a consequence of a combination of social developments that have undermined its coherence and credibility. (Waite, 2009, p 1)

The report advocates the need to combine recognition of the reality and value of social diversity with a firm commitment to a common citizenship, grounded in concepts of equality in relation to racial justice. It calls for programmes and opportunities for dialogue between residents and practitioners.

The definition of social control needs to be stretched beyond a focus on criminality and offending to engage with issues of hostility, tension and violence in communities. The experiences of Northern Ireland and of those towns in northern England that have had to respond to the rise of the far-right point to the need to locate the analysis of social control and community development within the dilemmas and challenges facing communities. Social control is as much about knowing how people can live together as it is about coping with crime and the fear of crime.

Discussing issues of social control can touch raw emotions. People living in oppressed circumstances can treat others as scapegoats very quickly, especially anyone who has a criminal record or who is seen as being different or as a threat. That is why, for example, the phenomenon of gangs in some urban areas, especially in parts of south London, is so alarming: disaffected people, mainly young men, form tight-knit gangs; they are alienated from adult society and are often in violent confrontation, including shootings, with other gangs and adults. Both rival gangs and adults often react to the violence not in any considered way but, more often than not, with comparable violence. Situations get out of control and actions, claims and counter-claims escalate. It need not be long before the basic building blocks of social control are eroded. Communities can turn against each other and turn in on themselves. This can occur, for example, with Travellers, as the following example shows.

Travellers in Westmeath, Ireland

In the summer of 2008, tensions between Traveller families in the Mullingar area grew to a point where homes were attacked and vandalised; there was a series of fights/ambushes and events happened at a pace beyond the capacity of the police to respond quickly and effectively. The knock-on effect was that Travellers from outside Mullingar were not prepared to access health services there, Traveller children were kept away from school and some Traveller families left the area and others planned to do so. In addition, families from the settled community who resided near members of the Traveller community asked to be moved because of fears for their own safety and that of their children. Westmeath Employment Pact, an independent organisation established to focus on employment opportunities and social inclusion, on behalf of the Westmeath Traveller inter-agency work, began to explore the feasibility of establishing a mediation service. It resourced an intervention between two families. While the presence of a mediator has had some impact, it has not ended the violence. The disarray caused by the feud within the Traveller community was mirrored within the various agencies working with Travellers and the standard response was based on health and safety concerns. (Westmeath Employment Pact, 2009, personal communication)

In addition to demonstrating the impact of conflict both within and between communities, this example shows how public services in such situations can be affected. A local presence of a service such as a housing office is reduced or done away with and fewer professionals are seen in the area. The combination of internal and external factors can lead to the fracturing of a community. Often the incidents and situation can be micro ones – between two or three families or between a few streets. It is not only the eye-catching events that result in social disorder and the inevitable review initiated by government and followed by the launching of a new programme. Unhealed wounds and enmities can lie beneath the surface for a long time, erupting only occasionally to upset the status quo.

Is a crisis-response approach – intervening in communities only in emergencies and when law and order are threatened overtly – an acceptable or sensible way to treat communities? Not only does such a 'fire brigade' attitude ignore the resources that exist in every community and that can be harnessed, it also stores up trouble for the future, re-enforcing the feeling within communities that government is remote and uncaring. Worse still, it carries the danger of setting up government as a monolithic state agency, prepared to invest in surveillance technology but unwilling to support processes needed to strengthen communities. Many people would argue that the logic of such a position leads to the erosion of civil liberties and to the introduction of legislation that in turn results in the accumulation of increased legal powers. The installation of increasing numbers of CCTV cameras on estates, in shopping malls and in parks is part of this dominance of state surveillance. There is a crime-reduction case for some CCTV but excessive reliance on this and other technology is, in the end, self-defeating because it creates a gulf between government and people, between state and society.

Any one of the issues summarised above – alienated young people, the clash of cultures and faiths and the danger of state hegemony – can bring communities to a tipping point, to the edge of disorder. Often communities demonstrate a surprising capacity to deal with disruption and difference. Drug dealing is an example: in some urban areas, residents are able to accept that dealing is taking place and do not insist on the dealers being hounded. Many people live in fear and the presence of 'pushers' is clear. Yet there can be a realisation among some community members of the need to be realistic. The acceptance is not defeatism but the result of pragmatism. There is, however, a line in the sand, as there is with prostitution. If the line of acceptability is, consciously or unconsciously, crossed, communities will turn against the perpetrators. Allegations of child abuse or child molestation bring out emotions and action that are much more clear-cut. It is in such situations that the issue of social control in communities becomes very stark. Our argument, however, is that the issue is present all of the time. Often hidden, sometimes surfacing only partially and briefly, social control is part of the mainstream agenda of communities. It is for that reason that community development has a key role to play.

Towards a model

The Safe and Sound project

Located in the heart of South Kilburn, London, and funded by the New Deal for Communities (NDC), the Safe and Sound project operates as a one-stop shop, offering crime reduction and crime prevention support to residents of all ages in a community significantly affected by drugs, violence and antisocial behaviour. Set up in 2003 by Crime Concern, the project aims to help tackle crime and the fear of crime in line with the NDC's crime reduction targets – to reduce the proportion of the population in fear of crime in South Kilburn to below 10 per cent by 2011.

The Safe and Sound project offers a range of community safety services, including home safety checks and security upgrades, personal safety classes and drugs and alcohol education. It is an example of one of the projects in the UK run by organisations such as Crime Concern and the National Association for the Care and Resettlement of Offenders

(NACRO) that have a clear crime prevention remit and that aim to create a safer, more inclusive society. Why is it that, for the most part, these projects are not fully recognisable as being mainstream community development? Why, indeed, can we not identify the community development elements in the work of youth offending teams or the community-based preventative strategies of most police forces?

Part of the answer is that these projects and approaches are focused on criminal justice. They are specialist interventions, whereas community development is generalist. The other, perhaps more significant part of the answer has to do with how we think about theory. Community development should be informed by a clear set of ideas that have been developed over time and that are seen to be valid. Otherwise, interventions will lack a central purpose and meaning. They will be pushed and pulled in different directions according to the policies and programmes of agencies and organisations. We are referring here not to abstract theory but to practice theory or practice principles – ideas that have been tested and that work on the ground. Using theory is a necessary condition for meaningful community development but it cannot become too abstract: it must be based on practice and remain relevant to it. The following model of community development and social control follows that approach and may help to give the approach a distinct identity. It consists of six concepts.

Joined-up thinking

Issues about social control cannot be addressed in isolation from other issues such as facilities for young people, recreation areas and the condition of the local environment and housing. The lives of individuals are made up of numerous connections and the same is true of communities. A community development approach needs to adopt a broad-brush approach if it is to succeed in mobilising a significant number of residents. It must appeal to the interests and concerns of a variety of community members, not be labelled as a specialised crime initiative. In that way it will have a chance of connecting with the informal networks and local associations that exist in every community:

> Getting people to work together who have different cultures, interest and social status is fraught with difficulties and tensions. Networks can be used to manage that plurality in very positive ways by building personal links and mediating between factions to overcome dogma and intransigence. It helps to demonstrate interest in other people and curiosity

about different lives and cultures. Good networking values diversity and deliberately seeks out experiences that will educate and challenge. (Gilchrist, 2004, p 82)

Alison Gilchrist's approach to networking is from a community development perspective. In the early community development literature, the word 'holistic' was used to refer to the all-embracing framework needed. Today we would use words such as 'cross-cutting', 'integrated' and 'joined up' to convey the essence of this central concept in community development.

Prevention

We noted at the beginning of the chapter the extent to which crime prevention is always high on the list of politicians' priorities. Community development's contribution to prevention is important, not because it can offer a panacea to crime but because it can bring a particular approach. Put simply, the concern is not just to prevent offending, but also to go back to the causes of offending and work on them. It is prevention that is central to community development and social control, not crime prevention as promoted by the police. Prevention is where community development's educative function becomes distinctive and it explains why the ideas of Paulo Freire have been so significant in community development theory. He calls the issues that generate natural energy within human beings 'generative themes'. The community development worker's role is to create a climate in which true dialogue can take place and this should take place in a cycle of reflection and action:

> At all stages of their liberation, the oppressed must see themselves as people engaged in the vocation of becoming more fully human. Reflection and action become essential. True reflection leads to action but that action will only be a genuine *praxis* if there is critical reflection on its consequences. (Freire, 1972, p 41)

It is through engaging with local people on an educative basis that community development can lay the foundations for strengthening a community. It is an extremely challenging and lengthy process. If, however, the process is effective, crime prevention will also become apparent.

Dialogue

While in the minds of some people community development equates with conflict, even confrontation, its essential purpose is to facilitate communication between people. If there is disagreement or conflict of interest, 'getting people to talk' becomes doubly important. Sometimes community development will support campaigns and direct action because circumstances point to the need for such methods to be used. The purpose, however, will be to open up dialogue between factions, notably between community groups and key local organisations and agencies – the local authority, partnership bodies and so on – and between young people and adults. In the criminal justice context, community development will seek to facilitate dialogue between different community groups and the police, magistrates and other criminal justice professionals. We noted earlier that one of the recommendations made by Mike Waite in his report on diversity and citizenship is for dialogue:

> The development of frank and honest dialogue, which names, explores and addresses real differences and difficulties, will be a key tool for building up trust between people and greater confidence and skill in working through issues that generate dispute and conflict. Such discussions, in a context which allows 'difficult conversations' to take place, will not only help with the social management of community relations. More generally, they could have a positive effect in building up civic skills and a stronger social sense of shared stake, belonging and citizenship, with benefit to the quality of democratic life. (Waite, 2009, pp 4-5)

We can see from this how dialogue in the community development context seeks to reach out to the basis of community life. It touches on profound issues and is concerned with the process of building and strengthening the ties between people and organisations – without which communities will not work. It also brings into focus the symbiosis of community development and civil society, between community and democracy.

Supporting community groups

The accessibility and reliability of a community development worker is crucial for networks and groups during the stage of formation when a community group is being set up. It is a necessary element of the model. Henderson and Thomas explore in detail what is involved in forming and building community groups, the movement from:

> ... an informal group of individuals meeting tentatively to test out each others' interests, commitment and general compatibility, and the deliberate formation of an organisation which has specified tasks to carry out and which has some kind of constituency. (Henderson and Thomas, 2002, p 134)

It is a key stage in the neighbourhood work process, requiring the community development worker to sustain his or her presence with patience, courage and a high level of skill. The difference between this generic model and the model we are proposing for engagement with social control issues is that the latter will need to include a focus on criminal justice issues. It must integrate this specialist focus within the generic model. It would include the following:

- support for crime-prevention groups such as neighbourhood watch as well as generalist community groups;
- involvement with community-based alternatives to custody schemes and programmes designed to combat antisocial behaviour;
- support for ex-offenders who commit themselves to rehabilitation in the community context.

Gauging community capability

When working effectively, a community development worker will excel at keeping his or her pulse on the community, noting the emergence of a new network, discontent with a public service, anxieties about uncertainties and mood swings about crime and the fear of crime. It is the last of these that a worker who has social control as part of his/her brief will wish to monitor. One aspect of this will be assessing the level of understanding and tolerance among local people towards offending – at both a general level and in relation to particular offences such as drug abuse and antisocial behaviour. The concept of community capability is a useful theoretical tool to assist this process. It pinpoints the notion of a capable or viable community being when residents work together to improve their quality of life. A key aspect of this, which builds on the work of Schoenberg (1979), is the setting up of mechanisms to negotiate and enforce shared agreements or contracts about public roles and responsibilities. These would vary from community to community but would certainly include agreements about personal safety, the identification of strangers, the maintenance of common property, the disposal of rubbish and the behaviour of children and young people.

A community's capacity to organise, based on mutual trust and networks, is an essential condition for the achievement of safety. If agreed mechanisms are to work, the assumption of both community members and professional workers must be that they will act in ways that enhance people's autonomy, self-esteem and the ability to work together to solve common problems. Thus gauging a community's capability to address issues to do with social control is designed to unlock the positive potential within people. It is not a functional precondition for community development but a fundamental part of community development's philosophy about the possibilities for change and the scope for people to work together. This does not imply that people have to declare 'wholesale' membership to some community identity or ideal but rather that numerous opportunities for people to become involved with others are created. Some of these opportunities will undoubtedly come within the sphere of social control.

Making connections

Our final practice-theory concept brings us closer to the practice arena. We emphasised earlier the complexity of communities in contemporary society:

> Successful communities are characterised as much by weak and strong ties and people relate to many overlapping communities, each of which takes precedence at different times. Weak ties and overlapping networks give people choices within and beyond their locality. (Taylor, 2003, p 84)

The existence of social capital is what most differentiates safe and organised communities from unsafe and disorganised ones, a conclusion drawn originally by Jane Jacobs in her 1961 book *The death and life of great American cities* (Jacobs, 1961). Social capital must be built on different levels, not exclusively within the neighbourhood. There needs to be bonding between close-knit groups and bridging between people who have less in common:

> To build bridging social capital requires that we transcend our social and political and professional identities to connect with people unlike ourselves. (Putnam, 2000, p 411)

There is widespread recognition within community development of the value to be obtained from organising visits of community groups to neighbourhoods that have pioneered effective ways of organising themselves. Visits and exchanges can be between two communities in the same town or between community groups in different countries. The latter have taken place on several occasions between groups in Britain and Hungary. However, perhaps more challenging for community development is the idea of deprived communities making connections with communities that are better off and that are functioning well. The Church Urban Fund initiated such connections in the 1990s but it has not become a trend. There are two reasons for considering why it can be worthwhile: to enable deprived communities to learn about strategies and actions that they could deploy, and to reduce the sense of separation between the two kinds of communities. Initiatives to reduce the labelling or demonising of one community by another by visits and exchanges are to be welcomed. If they also provide opportunities for people to learn new ways of engaging with social control issues, they are doubly valuable.

What would the practice element of the model we have just outlined look like? What would be its distinctive features? Essentially, we are suggesting that it would be based on generic community development practice. We emphasise especially the importance of work being undertaken at the grassroots – partnership work between organisations is only one dimension. Underpinning the generic approach, however, would be a commitment to focus on social control issues and a capacity to engage with programmes and systems that derive from the criminal justice system. Accordingly, we would expect practitioners to have knowledge and experience of this system and to be able to work confidently with it. Given the challenging nature of their work, we would also expect them to have conflict resolution and mediation skills.

Social control in the Hungarian context

In Hungary, community development professionals attach particular importance to the following two features of social control:

- the value/norm-forming role of communities and, therefore, the need to strengthen them so that the anomic state of society can be addressed;
- civil society's level of organisation, that is, to what extent can it take part in preparing for and making decisions and contributing to their implementation? What can community development do to enable local communities to practise the community function of control?

These two areas do not touch on the criminal justice agenda as discussed in the UK context. They do, however, connect with the case being made in this chapter for a wider definition of social control and the central part that community development can play in engaging with such a definition.

Hungarian society, like many other countries, is experiencing anomie: traditional norms and rules have fragmented and there are no new ones to replace them. In such situations, the rules of social coexistence become confused and norms fail to influence the behaviour of individuals.

In relation to democracy, it is important to be aware of the enormous social learning process that has taken place since the political transformation of Hungary. One of the many positive impacts of this process is that it highlights both the presence and nature of anomie. There is debate today as to who is responsible for what, with institutions trying to identify their spheres of activity. Yet society keeps being confronted with phenomena such as, for example, extreme ways of practising the right of assembly, and these shed light on the limitations of the law and other institutions. The public realises that laws by themselves cannot regulate frameworks for living together in ways that promote reassurance and community confidence. For this, norms would be needed that are based on common consent and that are respected by people – just as most people obey the law.

The lack of common norms highlights the value/norm-forming role of the institutions, organisations and networks that play a key role in socialisation: the family, school, groups and communities. A research project that examined how teachers choose their values could not find a latent structure or any guiding principles behind how educators select their values. This means that some educational principles appear in the thinking of teachers in an atomised way, not along lines represented by the society of educators as a whole. The research found this to be connected with the 'lack of orientation' in large segments of the population. People have no guidance in their lives (Paksi and Schmidt, 2006).

The extension of democracy is difficult because, over the past 20 years, norms and values have not been articulated in ways that would connect with the new social order, democracy and the market economy and that could therefore serve as a basis for civil control. These values would cover freedom, democracy and civil society; community, participation and self-organisation; self-help, self-control and enterprise; cooperation, solidarity and partnership.

From the community development perspective, the greatest problem is posed by individualism and the low priority given to public affairs. This is shown in two regional research studies on social capital (Vercseg, 2004) and the quality of human resources in Hungary respectively (Mészáros and Vercseg, 2006). The pursuit of individual enterprise predominates and social capital appears in social and community life as a private rather than a public good (Matějů, 2004). This hinders the renewal of communities and exacerbates the sense of 'drift' in people's lives. However, within this void, there may be the seeds of change:

> The emphasis on the values associated with individual freedom, their excessive dominance and the lack of a system of norms and frameworks may – as a result of having to confront their consequences – result in people expressing a desire for norms and frameworks. This, in turn, could mean that community solidarity, community action and co-operation are given an increasing significance. On the basis of this, one can assume that local communities will play a much greater role in the future. (Harkai, 2006, p 40)

In Chapter Six, the individual, community and political levels of participation were discussed. We touched on the issue of involvement in preparing for, making and implementing decisions. We also pointed to the complexity of the knowledge and skills base needed for civil society to become a real partner in decision-making processes.

When considering the practical implementation of values and investigating the situation of civil advocacy in Hungary, we know that civil society organisations are much less active in the area of advocacy and civil control than in the area of social participation. Organisations undertaking advocacy account for only about 15 per cent of all not-for-profit organisations:

The significant actors of advocacy and power control are usually not-for-profit organisations that are active in the area of environmental conservation, local development, legal protection and public security. To some extent, not-for-profit alliances can also be classified as part of this range, although the related lobbying is often organised as nationwide advocacy and does not focus on concrete local issues (Péterfi, 2009).

A researcher (Kuti, 1998, p 145) has identified the following four techniques for exerting influence on decision making:

Enforcement: this is a gentle form of 'blackmailing'. It can entail the 'squeezing' of alternative solutions into public or local governmental services in relation to different supplier and servicing roles.

Open advocacy of the 'initiative' type: these are forms of self-organisation within professions, for example:

- sectoral organisations connected to nature and environmental protection;
- civil coalitions (civil round tables, citizen councils) at local levels;
- advocacy and lobbying situations connected to specific social problems or crises.

Civil initiatives usually connect to issues on which decisions have not been made. Civil recommendations, for example, are made that target the passing of new laws or measures. Also related are the areas of public accountability and the enforcement of legislation through court or constitutional procedures. This kind of advocacy is often practised by the Hungarian Civil Liberties Union and Amnesty International.

Open advocacy of the 'defensive' type: this technique can be used when, prior to a decision, no process of negotiation, reconciliation and evaluation has begun with the involvement of all stakeholders. Typical examples are:

- the closure of schools or post offices in small villages and the cutting of bus or train services;
- the introduction of industries considered by local people either to be dangerous, such as a waste disposal or nuclear power plant, or unwelcome, such as covering free urban spaces and green areas with parking lots;
- the protection of the built environment in the Jewish district of Budapest, the introduction of urban regeneration programmes and the installation of a NATO base.

The strategy of integration: this is when there is formal integration of civil advocacy into decision making.

In Hungary, the involvement of civil society organisations in decision-making processes is regulated by a number of laws, including the constitution itself. The act on legislation, for example, declares that the social organisations concerned must be involved in the process of preparing legislation. According to the law on regional development, civil society organisations can form councils and take part in the work of regional councils. The act on the freedom of electronic information has also strengthened the position of civil society organisations. From the perspective of community development and social reconciliation, it is essential to extend the principles of the 1998 Aarhus Convention (UN Economic Commission for Europe) on access to information, public participation and access in environmental matters to include issues outside environmental decision making. It will require a considerable extension of skills:

> When looking for possible ways to achieve a better articulation of interests, a more productive advocacy and a more effective social control, we need to establish conditions that allow the development of these skills by citizens and their communities. (Péterfi, 2009, p 92)

Long-term processes require a way of living that stems from a profound commitment to democracy and active citizenship. Such a commitment can only be developed as a result of the value and norm-forming activities of communities and the democratic and community socialisation process described in Chapter Four.

EIGHT

Mutual support and solidarity

The concept of mutual support is frequently linked to community care, helpfully opening up a wider understanding of care in the community. At the same time, Warren connects mutual support with Durkheim's notion of 'organic solidarity ... a type of interdependence in interaction' (Warren, 1963, p 196). The concepts of mutual support and solidarity are therefore grounded in a tradition of powerful ideas. These in turn connect strongly with community development and civil society.

In the practice field, research undertaken in Scotland on community care and community development concluded that it was inappropriate to use a narrow definition of community care. A significant number of the local people and community development workers interviewed said that they experienced and articulated their involvement in providing support within a social inclusion framework. This led the researchers to conclude that the issue of caring communities must form part of corporate policymaking rather than being left to the social work/social services department (Barr et al, 2001). Commitment to using social justice and social inclusion as frameworks underpinning government and local authority policies has always been strong in Scotland. As a result, a body of experience has accrued from which other countries can learn. Rather than thinking of community care as being concerned, traditionally, with client groups of older people, people with mental health problems and people with physical or sensory impairments, a community development approach to community care seeks to connect the needs of vulnerable people with wider community issues and networks.

Our purpose in this chapter is twofold:

- to argue for the need to reposition community care within the mainstream of community development policy and practice. Caring for others is a necessary part of any definition of a strong community, yet currently it is marginal to community development;
- to explore the question of how communities can develop and maintain a commitment to mutual support and solidarity.

We begin by placing community care and solidarity in historical and contemporary contexts. We then summarise two case studies of community development approaches to community care and solidarity. These provide the basis for setting out 'ground rules' or principles of good practice with which politicians, policymakers, community development organisations and leaders of civil society need to engage if they are to embed the idea of community care genuinely and effectively in and with communities.

Context

We noted in Chapter Three how, historically, community development has had significant connections with social work. In the US and the UK, writers identified community work as one of three key methods in social work, the other two being casework and group work (Ross, 1955). This theoretical link was complemented operationally in the UK from the early 1970s by the appointment of community development workers to social services and social work departments. The ties between social work and community development weakened in the UK from the early 1980s (despite a short-lived interest, within social work, in the idea of community social work), but we should not underestimate their continuing significance after this period in other countries. Interestingly, as community development's fortunes in the UK social work context waned, its presence in the health sector began to be established. Community development's position in the latter increased in importance subsequently and remains significant today.

The social work connection resulted in the community development profession gaining experience of using its knowledge and skills to engage with community care issues. As community development came to operate increasingly in the context of regeneration and economic development, this resource was in danger of being ignored. We need to remember, however, the depth of the tradition of recognising and using informal social networks for the benefit of those people in need of care who are living in the community. Recognition comes from an influential sociological tradition of studying communities and their capacity to respond to care issues. Philip Abrams and others were successful in bringing evidence from this tradition to the attention of policymakers (Abrams et al, 1989) to the extent that the concept of 'social network' came into wider use (Bulmer, 1987).

The importance of social networks, relationships and social capital has since been widely recognised. However, not all relationships in the community are beneficial. Early community studies were heavily criticised for having virtually ignored the subordinate position of women in the home and the extent to which many communities, portrayed as exhibiting warmth and solidarity, were often very different when viewed from the inside:

> These were communities of oppression and the bonds of solidarity were the bonds of resistance. (Pahl, 1995, p 20)

Nevertheless, the potential of communities to support themselves and to care for friends and neighbours continues to be recognised, particularly when the energy and resourcefulness of 'insiders' (active local people) in community life is complemented by the input of 'outsiders' (recently settled residents). Thus the significance of the social network concept can be observed today. In his study of neighbouring and older people, for example, Kevin Harris writes about the accretion of 'unremarkable' little acts of recognition for others:

> These acts not only provide reassurance; taken together, they contribute to a sense of shared responsibility that, in turn, affords action in time of need. When people face a crisis, it is harder to mobilise them if they are disconnected. In the same way, it is harder to generate neighbourly support without a basis of recognition. (Harris, 2008, p 6)

The natural friendships, contacts and networks that are present in communities provide fertile ground where community development can contribute to community care. Over the past 15 years, there have been a number of attempts made to re-establish this potential within community development practice. In the early 1990s, the Community Development Foundation (CDF) produced a series of case studies to illustrate the connections between community development and community care, using them to advocate 'putting the community into community care'. Six themes were identified:

- knowing about community strengths – mapping needs and resources as an essential first step to working with community groups;
- helping communities prepare for community care – informal training and dialogue with local people in order to reduce popular anxieties about people in need of care;
- empowering community groups – helping to establish peer groups, enabling participation in decision-making forums and facilitating community enterprise, all aimed at enhancing self-determination;

- enhancing community support and networks – using community development techniques to facilitate positive networks;
- contracting out services – enabling community development workers to increase opportunities for devolving services to small organisations through capacity building;
- training for social services and social work staff to promote understanding of local communities (Armstrong and Henderson, 1992).

The Joseph Rowntree Foundation and the then Scottish Office funded CDF to produce a training pack and to undertake action research with four local authorities in Scotland. In addition to connecting community care with social inclusion, the action research project demonstrated that:

> Community development and community care can have common interests and potentially mutual benefits. Methods of community development can help achieve the objectives of progressive community care, whilst engagement with user communities helps community development to realise its vision of inclusiveness. (Barr et al, 2001, p 4)

Journal articles and evaluation reports explored the connections between community development and community care (Lloyd and Gilchrist, 1994; Barr et al, 1998; Sharkey, 2000; Quilgars, 2002). From 2002, CDF and the Sainsbury Centre for Mental Health formed a partnership in order to take forward community development ideas and practice in the mental health field. This produced useful outcomes, notably practice conferences in Brighton and Bradford that identified common ground between a range of community care and community development practitioners. At the policy level, the National Social Inclusion Programme at the Care Services Improvement Partnership commissioned CDF to review the relevant literature and undertake a survey and interviews with a mix of community development and mental health professionals and with people with experience of mental ill health. The authors of the report identify tensions between mental health and community development work but they reaffirm the potential of community development practice for making a valuable contribution in the field of mental health:

> Community development practitioners helped mental health staff to improve their services for diverse communities and worked to improve mental health awareness within

generic services. They developed structures, processes and skills for public participation, sometimes in creative, innovative ways. The appreciation of commissioners and participants demonstrated the impact of their achievement. (Seebohm and Gilchrist, 2008, p 10)

We draw on the above study when, in the chapter's final section, we put forward guiding principles for community development's contribution to community care. What conclusions can be drawn from our summary of work undertaken over recent years on community development and community care? Has it led to increased recognition by policymakers and commissioners of the potential of community development in the community care context or is the topic still on the margins of the agendas of both community care policymakers and the community development profession? The two case studies that follow throw some light on these questions.

Case studies

Sharing Voices Bradford

Sharing Voices Bradford (SVB) is a mental health project that uses community development principles and methods, based in a densely populated inner-city area of Bradford. It was set up in 2002 with funding from Bradford Primary Care Trust and was supported by the Centre for Citizenship and Community Mental Health at the University of Bradford. It has worked with a wide range of local and national mental health and other organisations.

The project's origins lay in the commitment to explore how a critical perspective in mental health could be put into practice. This came about as a result of two psychiatrists in Bradford becoming aware of the negative experiences that people from black and minority ethnic (BME) communities were likely to have when using mental health services compared with their white counterparts. The psychiatrists contacted CDF to ensure that community development principles and methods would be central to the project.

During the first three years, the project employed two community development workers, a team leader and an office manager. The team has now expanded and the project works with all Bradford's BME communities, including asylum seekers and refugees. Individuals with mental health difficulties have played a central part in the project's activities and the project has promoted an ethos of peer support, mutual aid and public participation. The community development staff have helped to set up and support a variety of community groups, self-help and peer groups, including Hamdard, a group for Muslim women; Creative Expressions, a group for women wanting to express themselves through the arts; a fitness group for men of any ethnicity or faith; a music group for men and women of any faith; and other support groups specifically for South Asian women. The project has built up a group of volunteers, many of whom have had experience of the mental health system.

Over the initial three-year period, SVB:

- enabled people from diverse communities to set up groups where they could address shared experiences of distress in their own way;
- supported individuals to develop their social, spiritual and economic potential;
- developed partnerships and support networks that increased capacity in the statutory, voluntary and community sectors and widened access to support for people from BME communities;
- increased BME participation in service design and delivery and other local issues in statutory and voluntary forums;
- signposted people who needed resources to the statutory and voluntary sector;
- advocated choice and citizenship in dialogue and debate on non-medical understandings of distress.

SVB is committed to the ongoing evaluation of its work. In 2003, it obtained funding from three national charities to undertake a nine-month participatory action research programme. The report on the process that took place provided recommendations for strengthening the project (Seebohm et al, 2005). It also discusses issues that have relevance beyond the Bradford context:

- Community development at SVB involves a combination of safe spaces and networks that extend outwards, linking the mental health field with sports, leisure, arts and local organisations. Understanding of mental ill health is increased and stigma reduced as organisations become more inclusive. The networks have led to an increase in social capital and community cohesion.
- The research evidence on the value of peer support and mutual aid in promoting recovery from mental ill health is strong and further supported by SVB's work.
- By tapping into the expertise of 'experts by experience' and BME communities, stigma is tackled more effectively and the benefits for

the individuals involved, their communities and the National Health Service (NHS) can be considerable.
- Primary care trusts can choose to be ambitious ('radical') or more cautious, but they need to manage the expectations of their staff and communities accordingly.

The style of community development that characterises SVB reflects its mental health remit. More work is done with individuals than is normal within generic community development projects and it works closely with the statutory providers of mental health services. That is why SVB was selected as a case study: it carries out a clear community care function, but does so within a community development framework. It also works within the public sector context, seeking especially to open up genuine possibilities for participation in the NHS for mental health service users from BME communities. A community research process undertaken for SVB by the International Centre for Participation Studies at the University of Bradford uncovered a number of key issues that discourage or prevent participation:

> In setting up participation processes, service providers need to think about where decisions will actually be taken and by whom, and how the process will deal with tensions and disagreements, for example instances in which communities want to move in different directions to the established thinking in the health service. (Blakey, 2005, p 5)

SVB has demonstrated a capacity to engage at both grassroots and policy levels and to draw in partner organisations locally and nationally. The project is unusually well documented. More significantly, it has taken a stance on the mental health needs of BME communities that means it is contributing to an area of policy and practice that has been seriously neglected.

Solidarity: whose responsibility?

The Civil College Foundation (CCF), a community development training organisation described in Chapter Ten, opened its training centre in 1997. The former elementary school is situated in the middle of a small farming area called Kunbábony. The settlement has 400 inhabitants and is approximately 50 miles south of Budapest.

The opening of CCF stimulated local community life and a local association was formed to organise cultural and leisure activities. The Hungarian Association for

Community Development (HACD) and CCF initiated a small regional community development process and this has continued since.

In 1998, the local association of Kunbábony submitted a proposal to the 'Small Gardens' programme of the Autonomy Foundation, which supplies good-quality sowing seed for disadvantaged families. The proposal was successful but the project created conflict within the association and the membership divided into two camps. One held that tackling social problems was not the responsibility of the organisation ('Nobody gives us anything for free!'). The other insisted that it was one of the tasks of the organisation because the community's quality of life would not improve as long as local people failed to support each other and ignored other people's problems.

Following lengthy considerations, the association decided to provide 30 poor families with the opportunity to produce the vegetables they needed in their gardens. The organising was done by the association: members assessed needs, then purchased and distributed the necessary seeds, fertilisers and pesticides and one of the members, an agricultural professional, provided advice for the families. The programme was implemented successfully.

Even though the project entailed conflict, there was solidarity in the end. The association's membership was divided to such an extent that the organisation stopped functioning for several years. It was re-established in 2004, elected a new leadership and since that time all the members agree that striving for the common good is among the responsibilities of the organisation, including visiting and caring for elderly and sick people living in remote, isolated farms. The community needed this much time to understand the new situation, to identify newly emerging problems and to get involved in solving them.

In spite of the extended conflict, development work helped community members understand an important message brought by the political transformation of Hungary: solidarity and taking responsibility for each other are issues that should not to be dealt with exclusively by the state or local authorities but also by citizens themselves.

Chapter Three shows how, prior to the political transformation in Hungary, a form of mechanical solidarity existed. It had been inherited from the semi-traditional, pre-Second World War society and was accompanied by a 'collective consciousness'-building efforts and social organisation methods of the soviet-type system. In this system, solidarity was built from above. Although Hungary still faces the consequences of pseudo-equalitarianism and limited participation, it can be argued that in the state party system no officially endorsed and acknowledged ethnic-based discrimination existed either in terms of the labour market or of involvement in local communities.

Collective solidarity based on common awareness has weakened in all modern societies, but in central and eastern Europe it collapsed as a result of political transformation. This does not mean that solidarity disappeared completely because people in the region have always been active in providing support, voluntary work and donations when natural disasters or armed conflicts occur. The provision of mutual support between neighbours has also, up to a point, continued. But solidarity with 'others', those who are 'not from among us', does not seem to be functioning sufficiently (Rorty, 1989). The radically changed social and community context has created great uncertainty and this has undermined people's confidence, resulting in a cessation of the earlier practice of mutual support. It was not only the speed and force of the changes that altered the conditions of practising solidarity. The other factor was competition. This replaced solidarity with conflict, making cooperation increasingly problematic.

What do the case studies, the summary of UK practice and the place of solidarity in Hungarian civil society, tell us about the current scope, as well as the potential, of using community development to support mutual aid and solidarity? In the UK context, there is evidence that doors into the policy arena are being prised open. SVB's example of drawing on community development principles was followed by the Department of Health (DH) committing itself to the appointment of 500 community development workers to work in mental health contexts as part of its action plan to address negative experiences of people from BME communities (DH, 2005). While there have been recruitment and managerial problems with the programme (Walker and Craig, 2009), its announcement was evidence of recognition by policymakers of community development's potential contribution to community care, at least within the mental health field.

The collaboration between CDF and the National Social Inclusion Programme on a study of mental health and community development (Seebohm and Gilchrist, 2008) suggests that there may now be awareness among community development organisations of the community care issue. There is, however, still some way to go. Much has been done in the past few years on the relationship between community development and mental health, but this needs to be complemented by parallel work with organisations concerned with the needs of older people and those with physical and sensory impairments. There has been an accumulation of a range of practice experience and this has led to the strengthening of practice development. This now has to be taken to a new level, with the inclusion of the policy and organisational dimensions.

In Hungary, and probably in most other central and eastern European countries, the issue of seeking to bring together community development and community care as it is defined in the UK context is not apparent, at least not yet. Rather, the concern is to rediscover the sense of solidarity between citizens, to care for each other not just in terms of the welfare of vulnerable people but also as neighbours. Accordingly, the theme of mutual support and solidarity forms part of a generic community development agenda rather than an offshoot or specialised area. While this makes comparison between the UK and Hungarian contexts difficult, it does not mean that we have to depend on only one of them to formulate guiding principles. On the contrary, the differences between them help to deepen the principles and ensure that they can be made applicable in a variety of contexts.

Guiding principles

In this concluding part of the chapter, we set out seven practice principles that we believe should inform the planning and practice required for a community development approach to community care. They reflect our analysis of the practice experiences that have been discussed in this chapter. They are put forward in order to ensure that a community development approach to community care has a definite identity, not out of concern for any mythical purity of community development but because of the need to be clear about what it can contribute to building and supporting mutual aid and solidarity.

Taking a distinctive approach

It is important to separate a community development approach to community care from other approaches such as community service, volunteering and the support provided by local authorities, health agencies and voluntary organisations for vulnerable people. Often it is partnerships between these bodies that provide support. Support, community development, community service and volunteering are all closely connected and each of them makes invaluable contributions to sustaining people's lives in locality, identity and interest communities. Our insistence on the need to recognise community development as a distinct approach comes from having observed how community development's impact can become diluted because it has not been defined and specified sufficiently rigorously. Its use as a catch-all term can result in it being given goals and objectives that are too broad, with the result that it is not effective. Precisely because working with communities means being pulled in different directions and being subject to a variety of pressures, the need to plan, remain focused and evaluate community development interventions is particularly important.

Building on strengths

We drew attention at the beginning of the chapter to the rich community resources of self-help, mutual aid and informal networks. Michael Hill argues for the nurturing of networks of care as being necessary for caring relationships alongside caring services:

> But this cannot be done 'top down' by politicians, telling us what our obligations are to each other, but through the recognition of real communities of interest that, in our complex world, will not have a simple spatial identity. (Hill, 2007, p 17)

Community development must take heed of this argument and ensure that it identifies and builds on existing networks both between and within neighbourhoods. It is easy to fall into the trap of either assuming that the caring is done on a neighbour-to-neighbour basis or that informal caring networks are not relevant to community development. Both assumptions are misguided.

Distinguishing between service delivery and community development

There are two points here, both of them important. First, community development risks becoming nothing if it forms part of the delivery of care services. Community development is about enabling people to act together and it is concerned to bring about, or respond to, social change. If community care programme managers attempt to use it as part of their responsibility to deliver services, they misunderstand community development's purpose. Community development can certainly be used to improve delivery by, for example, advising services on how to reach out to isolated or excluded community members and by facilitating contact with relevant community organisations and networks. Neither of these, however, equates with community development being part of service delivery.

Second, the user-involvement movement that, over the past two decades, has greatly extended its influence on service providers is clearly relevant to community development. Both argue the case for participation and in doing so make use of the same theories and models. Their functions, however, are different and, rather than be tempted to interchange them, it is important to be aware of the extent to which the one can build on the other. One of the findings from the action research carried out in Scotland and referred to earlier was evidence of how service users are not simply recipients of services; often they are also community leaders:

> There had to be a flexible appreciation of the user/leader relationship and recognition that being a potential or actual service user is not necessarily an impediment to being an effective community leader. (Henderson, 2001, p 23)

The action research also noted the importance of the focus of users' participation not being seen to be restricted to the specific services provided within community care. Their participation reflected a wider demand for issues to be addressed across a range of dimensions of their lives. This finding connects with one of the key themes running through all the chapters, namely the generic nature of community development and its concern to keep agendas broad rather than allow them to be narrowed down.

Working on a one-to-one basis

The SVB case study brings out the significance of work undertaken with individuals within a mental health and community development project. We believe there is a similar significance for projects working with older people and people who have physical and sensory impairments. Why does one-to-one work need to characterise a community development approach to community care? Is there not a danger of it diluting community development principles, of pulling practice away from work with community groups and networks? There is undoubtedly a risk of this happening; often a project will find itself performing a delicate balancing act between, on the one hand, being seen exclusively as a referral point for individuals and, on the other, as being uninterested in the plight of individuals. A key criterion for the success of such a project is the extent to which it achieves the balance between these two extremes.

The reason why work with individuals has to take place alongside collective work is that the needs of vulnerable people require individual attention. Practitioners have to be available to work in confidence with individuals who have support needs. This resource should be stated clearly by a community development project, not kept in the background. In that way, individuals who normally might never cross the threshold of a community project can have the confidence to do so. They can then decide if they want to become involved in a project's other activities, whether these are within the project's building or out in the community.

The validity of making work with individuals a key part of a community development approach to community care indicates the importance of learning from practice experiences and case studies. If these are found consistently to support the argument being put forward here, practitioners can be assured of the validity of the approach. A last point to note: it is not as if generic community development does not work on a one-to-one basis. On the contrary, a good community development worker will spend considerable periods of time working with individuals, for example, to encourage them to become involved with a group or to take on a leadership role.

Working in partnership

Community development workers who practise in the community care field have to invest time in working with statutory, voluntary and private sector organisations; they need to communicate with health and social work staff about the work they are doing. More often than not, they also need to enter into agreements with organisations about their respective work responsibilities and decide which of these are best undertaken together and which separately. Partnership working is one of the guiding principles informing community development and community care because at the centre of the work is concern for vulnerable individuals who are either already receiving services or whose situation requires that they do so. This perspective on partnership needs to be understood alongside the wider framework of partnership that 'has become the currency of policy-making in countries across the world' (Taylor, 2003, p 114).

Evidence from research and practice tells us that, in the community development context, partnership working is problematic because it puts pressures on overstretched community groups and because power generally lies with the large organisations within a partnership. Nevertheless, the need for partnership working in the care context is compelling. Furthermore, it can lead to improved working relationships between different kinds of practitioners. Patience Seebohm and Alison Gilchrist report that 'Multi-agency forums seemed to work well, confirming that community development can support partnership working to meet mental health needs' (Seebohm and Gilchrist, 2008, p 57).

An important implication of partnership working is the need to build in learning opportunities for individuals, groups and networks, especially between members of user and community groups, practitioners and managers. They share common interests and goals, but usually use different methods and have access to different resources.

Making connections

It is essential that work in the area under discussion looks outwards to a wider agenda, especially to social justice and social inclusion issues. There is a risk of being drawn into the particular perspectives of agencies. This is especially damaging for people from non-western communities. However, for all those people labelled as sick or inadequate, community development can help by making them aware of the social and economic determinants of ill health so that they can escape from individual shame and guilt. Community development can also provide opportunities for members of groups and networks to raise care issues in a wider context. Advocates and champions are needed as much within this wider context as they are within the care field itself. Community care connects with social justice and social inclusion in fundamental ways, as we have argued earlier, and making connections with these should form a key part of a community development approach to community care.

Achieving clarity

A skilled community development practitioner will not only be clear about goals, objectives and methods but also demonstrate clearly to local people what he or she is doing at any one time. This is done in order to help people understand what is happening, thereby building trust and commitment, and encourage community leaders and others to learn the skills and knowledge of community development. Using community development in the community care context requires this kind of openness and clarity; vulnerable people need to become familiar with the community development process and gain confidence in being part of it. Similarly, members of community groups will want to understand why a community development worker is encouraging them to engage with care issues in a neighbourhood or across a wider urban or rural area. Community leaders especially can play a crucial part in helping to make connections between a range of community activities and responding to care issues – they are the people who can convene community interests, act as conduits for ideas and as catalysts for new initiatives. The worker will need to be able to explain both the policy and organisational aspects of community care and the nature of the problems experienced by people with mental health problems, older people and those with physical and sensory impairments. The importance of this educative role by a community development worker should not be underestimated.

Underpinning all of the above principles is self-determination, enabling people to come together to pursue their own goals. These may relate to their care services and so be connected with the user movement. Or their priorities may relate to other issues, such as transport, the environment or the arts. The essential point is that community development can shift the locus of control and power from service provider to the user or community.

Putting guiding principles into practice can inform the long haul of extending the contribution of community development to processes of strengthening the bonds of mutual support and solidarity. In their influential framework for evaluating community development, Alan Barr and Stuart Hashagen identify a caring community as one of the essential quality-of-life dimensions of a healthy community:

> One of the most important characteristics of a strong
> community is the nature of the support and care it offers
> its members. (Barr and Hashagen, 2000, p 39)

Alongside the re-stating of this argument and its application at community, organisational and policy levels, we need to recall that there is an urgency attached to the focus of this chapter:

• There is clear evidence of the increasing burdens being placed on carers, particularly given the increasing numbers of older people in most countries' populations. The pressures on individuals and families who are carers inevitably affect informal networks in communities and their capacity, as well as their potential, to give mutual support and solidarity.

- The cost of providing social care in the UK has been estimated by Hirsch (2005) to be £14.2 billion and he thinks that this could quadruple by the middle of this century. Whether or not such expenditure is sustainable is questionable and, on the assumption that some commitment to universalist principles will be maintained, the case for organisations to adopt community development strategies could become increasingly evident.
- Despite the 2008/09 economic recession and its long-term impact on public expenditure, citizens' increased expectations of their quality of life are likely to continue to rise. There will therefore be pressures on governments, as well as statutory, voluntary and private sector organisations, to ensure acceptable standards of care. This could be another reason why policymakers and managers may turn to community development.

These future scenarios need to be part of the community development and community care framework. There is an increasing literature on how wellbeing and 'flourishing' individuals and groups are dependent on mutual support and solidarity (Friedli, 2009). In policy terms, there are growing calls for a more social Europe and for responses to the global financial crisis that test alternative economic and social models. These developments are a significant backdrop to the arguments put forward in this chapter. They remind us that the contribution of community development to mutual support and solidarity should not be seen as a specialist concern but rather as belonging to a rich and lively set of ideas and debate.

NINE

The potential of community development

Is community development sufficiently well equipped to deliver successful outcomes in the context of civil society and the challenges of the 21st century? That is the question we explore in this chapter. It is a pivotal chapter for three reasons: it expands on the five ways in which, in Chapter Two, we argue that community development can help communities to become part of civil society (challenging, defending, maintaining, recognising and strengthening civil society); it draws on the ideas presented in Chapters Four to Eight; and it anticipates the authors' conclusions. By presenting first a Hungarian and then a UK perspective on community development's potential, the different emphases and meanings given to the concept of civil society can also be acknowledged. In a brief final section, we draw attention to the similarities and differences between the two perspectives.

A Hungarian perspective

A profession can never be satisfied with the results achieved in the past; it has to look for new directions and methods on a continuous basis. This is particularly true when a profession sets an arena for intervention that is broader and more comprehensive than anything before − civil society. We begin by reflecting on community development and the nature of change in the context of civil society.

Community development changes as society changes. It is constantly looking for areas where its special kind of intervention can be applied. In numerous areas its track record points to its potential for exerting influence on society, through settlements and community/cultural centres, community education, anti-poverty programmes, participation, multiculturalism, regeneration, rural development, community economic development, social planning and, to an increasing extent, civil society and non-governmental organisations (NGOs).

Since community development and change are inseparable, the former is constantly challenged by the development of society and communities to find and, if necessary, modify its optimal scope of action. Why and how does change take place in professional perspectives?

- Change can occur when a threat arises that affects society as a whole, for example, a growing number of slums, an increase in the number of immigrants, an economic crisis or war. The need for developing civil society probably originates from two kinds of threats: the unsustainability of welfare systems and recognition that democracy is empty without a strong civil society. Citizens become indifferent and, due to the low level of participation, those in power increasingly fail to be legitimised.
- Change in the form of deterioration and decrease of social capital may be experienced as a milder threat. This process often remains 'invisible' for a long time, hiding the danger it may entail. But social leaders and other social stakeholders may be stimulated to take action when they realise that such indicators as people losing trust in each other and their public institutions, their inability to cooperate and the lack of social solidarity are interrelated.
- Sooner or later, changes will occur in the occupational categories that were established with one 'stroke of the pen' to demonstrate an ideological objective or political intention. Examples of this are former professions in central and eastern Europe that were created to spread the socialist ideology and the new culture, such as 'ideological officer', 'agitator-propagandist' and 'cultural worker'. All of these professions have now disappeared or undergone transformation. The same fate may await the occupational categories established by the European Union (EU) and national development centres to pursue development objectives (for example, rural development agencies, small regional bureaux and so-called equal opportunity centres).
- Change may be afoot when professions with a marginal situation in the social division of labour cannot prove their viability in a convincing way. One of the reasons for this is that the profession 'is not in the right place'. This means that it undertakes (mostly involuntarily) the solving or handling of problems for which it lacks the necessary tools or intellectual and infrastructural resources. The failures may lead to the formulation of new objectives and the development of new potential for action.
- Finally, change may occur in the vocational thinking of disciplines that are constantly seeking new scope for their action. In theory, all human service professions fall into this category, including community development.

Much depends on how quickly and flexibly the prevailing social leadership can react to new challenges and whether it is ready to deploy strategies and tools, such as community development, to accelerate social renewal and ensure its influence through the provision of legal, institutional and financial support.

Key questions

The concept of civil society gained new significance in Europe in the 1990s. It gave hope that democracy could be revived. Efforts to increase people's participation in their own affairs intensified. In the West, the usual explanation given for the changes cited the crisis of the welfare state and democracy, while in central and eastern Europe it related to the historic opportunity to build – partly rebuild – new civil society and democracies. Today, however, the emphasis has shifted towards seeing civil society as a service provider, and community development as an organiser of services. Both these perceptions raise concerns among many professionals.

It was at an international conference held in Budapest in 2004 and with the issuing of the Budapest Declaration that European community development was placed firmly in the context of civil society:

> Community development is a way of strengthening civil society by prioritising the actions of communities and their perspectives in the development of social, economic and environmental policy. It seeks the empowerment of local communities, taken to mean both geographical communities, communities of interest or identity and communities organising around specific themes or policy initiatives. It strengthens the capacity of people as active citizens through their community groups, organisations and networks; and the capacity of institutions and agencies (public, private and non-governmental) to work in dialogue with citizens to shape and determine change in their communities. It plays a crucial role in supporting active democratic life by promoting the autonomous voice of disadvantaged and vulnerable communities. It has a set of core values/social principles covering human rights, social inclusion, equality and respect for diversity; and a specific skills and knowledge base. (CEBSD/IACD/HACD, 2004, preamble)

The development of civil society is a strong idea that must remain accessible to ordinary people, not reified. It offers enormous scope. It facilitates development by local communities and is able to build on 'traditional' approaches to professional intervention in which community development has expertise, in the areas of disadvantage, participation and multicultural coexistence. Community development should counter any expectations of social leaders and communities that it can solve these problems on its own. The development of civil society covers the sharing of awareness and responsibility among all stakeholders of society through regular communication, empowerment processes, implementing the outcomes of training processes and the organisation of publicity. For the development of civil society, it is not always necessary to target marginalised or labelled groups of people. A civil society that is organised at a certain level looks for new solutions. It is willing to develop and will do so by itself.

Since it is only recently that European community development has started thinking in the context of civil society, the exploration of community development means that we have to address a number of fundamental questions, notably:

• Is community development sufficiently well equipped to deliver successful outcomes in the context of civil society?
• Community development has a critically important contribution to make, but is it capable of doing so? In particular, what is the 'state of health' of community development theory, practice theory and practice tools? Where are these strong and where are they weak?

As a result of its history and experiences, community development is able to specify methods and organisational structures for community intervention. It has established and developed theoretical frameworks, a practice theory and a methodology for professional intervention that is widely acknowledged and applied. In some countries, the training of professionals is built on a developed multi-level approach, offering a range of training courses from short adult education courses through different levels of vocational courses to higher education courses. Standards for community development are also developed on a regular basis. Thus community development has built up a professional institutional system that, in varying degrees, is supported by the public, NGO and private sectors.

International community development debates and outcomes (research and practice) are published widely, notably in the *Community Development Journal*. The membership of the International Association for Community Development spans all the continents. The Combined European Bureau for Social Development (CEBSD) represents the European continent. When a range of national organisations, international networks and national action plans established during the course of EU programmes are added, it can be seen that community development has become a key component of social development programmes.

In the context of civil society, community development should have an easier task than in earlier times because it does not have to adapt to the professional systems and procedures of other disciplines (education/ socialisation, economic development, social work, social planning). The need to be supported by another, more powerful, profession was often a burden for community development in the past. Today, community development has a chance to make the best use of its own theory and practice tools in the development of national and international civil societies.

Yet considerable difficulties manifest themselves around community development's effectiveness in the context of civil society, especially in the newly accessed EU states. In these countries, community development has not yet built up the structures, governing principles and mechanisms that could secure a steady development for the profession. The capacity of the Hungarian Association for Community Development (HACD) is still weak even after 20 years of existence. Being an association, it is part of the civil sphere itself and even though it has fought battles to secure its survival and sustainability, and make its voice heard and acknowledged, it is still unable to influence social development decision-making processes sufficiently and effectively. The Budapest Declaration provides evidence that this does not hold true only for Hungarian practice. European community development as a whole still has a lot to do in order for the profession to be well equipped to deliver successful outcomes in the context of civil society.

From the perspective of central and eastern Europe, the potential contribution of community development to the strengthening of civil society can be summarised as follows.

• Community development places the emphasis on taking the initiative and developing participation, which is the token of democracy's renewal. The Hungarian community development concept in use today emphasises this function of community development:

> The essence of community development is to develop the ability of local communities to take initiatives and action. This process involves action, active local citizens, their organisations and networks and – to an extent defined by local needs – community development professionals whose

encouraging/stimulating, informing and contact-organising activities can foster the establishment or strengthening of local community networks. (Varga and Vercseg, 1998, p 22)

These processes conform with the functions of the third or NGO sector, which is essentially civil society itself. The most important functions of civil society are taking initiatives and building new institutions in local communities.

- Community development has a specific methodology needed for developing civil society and working with volunteers. Community development involves people in networks of initiators and actors who would not be able to take initiatives or act for the common good on their own.
- The type of community action generated by community development builds self-confidence and brings new experiences in connection with social, community, organisational and networking issues.
- During the process of empowerment, community development tries to help people understand the meaning of civil existence and its scope for action. Through local action, it helps to clarify civil and community roles and their relation to the public and private sectors, communicating the importance of fulfilling these roles, representing interests and protecting human rights. Community development can help to ensure that human rights that are guaranteed by the constitution (for example, the rights to education and participation) cease to be merely declared and abstract directives but become everyday practice for local citizens. Often, the conditions for practising rights also need to be created and community development can play a major role in this process (for example, by including the excluded, ensuring the protection of human dignity, providing free access to adult education, organising social cooperatives). Community development can also facilitate the acquisition of civil action techniques, such as how to set up an association, how to prepare a charter, how to involve members, how to organise and run public meetings, how to write reports and how to organise a local event or campaign.

By itself, however, community development is unable to enforce its special contribution. Community and civil participation need to have both moral and practical support. This point is emphasised in the Budapest Declaration. Delegates acknowledged the priority being given by the EU to strengthening civil society and emphasised the important role that community development can play in supporting that process and in protecting the human rights of everyone. The declaration made recommendations for community development in nine crucial areas, all of which have a focus on developing participation and civil society: policy and legislation at European, national and local levels of government; training; theory and research; rural issues; urban regeneration; sustainable development and the environment; lifelong learning and cultural development; local economic development and the social economy; and minorities, migration, racism and discrimination.

In a supportive European and social environment, community development needs to take further steps in the context of civil society. It has to increase its flexibility and independence and, in the course of collaborating with civil society, it should also develop new theoretical frameworks and methods.

Citizen action can extend to all areas of life. Citizens do not think in terms of disciplines or pursuing their individual professional interests. Rather, they take local problems as a starting point and look for community-based solutions, incorporating knowledge from various disciplines in the process. The main point is to give free rein to critical thinking and community initiatives, encouraging alternatives and collaborative problem solving.

Community development is not a process exclusively generated by professionals. The key role is played by citizens not by professionals. In order for citizens to become the key 'players' in the community development process, they need to be able to manage the process themselves. That is where community development professionals have their role to play.

Flexibility and independence

Civil society's scope for generating action requires the highest level of flexibility and loyalty from community development professionals. These individuals need to adapt to all parts of the structures of local communities and be prepared to challenge existing community conditions. They need to be at ease with, and tolerant towards, open-ended situations and incomplete, reactive responses; to have patience in waiting for things to develop but also a constant wish to encourage organisation. All this requires knowledge of community development principles and theory, a belief that community development can deliver, self-knowledge, familiarity with a range of methods and a willingness to experiment.

The extent of the professional's independence is also a key issue and this is linked strongly to the aims and priorities of organisations that commission community development programmes. In Hungary, only a few professionals make a living from community development. In their case, one cannot talk about a group of professionals but rather about specialists who belong to different disciplines. For them, the concepts of community, civil society, participation and democracy carry unique significance. Accordingly, in shaping the role of their profession, they seek community-based solutions in community and cultural centres, youth, leisure and information centres, schools and family support centres as well as in civil organisations involved in legal and interest representation, nature conservation and environmental action and, more recently, in development projects. Hungary has striven for a long time to create a cohesive core of community development professionals. In the last few years, it has been conceded that it might not be such a bad thing if this cannot be achieved, for it would allow professionals to keep their independence.

In the case of state employees, the long-debated question of where professionals' loyalty should lie is clear. These professionals have few resources at their disposal and they are increasingly forced to boost their share of the state budget with funding from other sources. This makes their situation difficult. Inevitably, because their job is provided by the state, there are two deleterious effects on both civil society and vocational development: a reluctance to support innovation (What for? Who demands it?) and a requirement to show loyalty to their employer, namely local or national government. Interaction with civil society is most problematic when the effects can be traced back to other human service professions.

Civil society wants change while the public sector wants undiscerning acquiescence and collaboration (in the form of contracted services). Civil society gives rise to conflict because it wants change, while the public sector wants development without conflict. Civil society wants to interfere, but the public sector is unable to do anything with this interference because it wants to decide on its own. In the competition for contracts and projects, the candidates have to subordinate their goals to the priorities of the organisations that fund the projects. To put it simply, they 'sell themselves'. Thus their loyalty towards those who provide positions and contracts may be stronger than their loyalty towards members of the community.

One of the most effective solutions to the issue of independence is where sponsoring organisations (mostly national organisations and local authorities, donors from the business sector and funding bodies in the civil sector) sign a cooperation agreement for at least a three-year period. In such schemes, none of the partners has a decisive majority and a range of representatives from different human service professions are employed in the programme. In this way, decisions are made on the basis of a 'collective wisdom' or collective opinion. The other important advantage is that the schemes exclude quick, crude, result-oriented project-based initiatives. Instead, they produce genuine process-based, long-term results that are embedded and sustainable.

It would be desirable if funding programmes could give local community groups a chance to employ local community development professionals. This would secure the loyalty of professionals towards the community groups with which they work. When it becomes possible to employ professionals in this way, an entirely new kind of professional selection will emerge, one that highlights the role of the professional as a catalyst rather than one that is geared towards service provision. Clearly, this would have implications for the training of professionals.

New theoretical frameworks and methods

To have meaningful reflection on community development, there is a need for the constant renewal of theoretical frameworks. Basic principles are an essential part of frameworks. They are the starting point for all professions and provide a basis for comparison. Everything that happens within the parameters of the profession is deemed good or bad, exemplary or discardable, in relation to these basic principles. When selecting the fundamental principles, we must, therefore, be certain that they reflect important values. The latter can change alongside the shifting focus of community development.

The community and its modern medium, civil society, rarely appear among the basic principles of community development, even though together they form the most profession-specific principle of the discipline. The reason for this is that basic principles are usually drawn from practice, not from 'grand theories' about community and civil society. At the same time, it should be noted that the widely recognised basic principles of community development, such as social justice, equality, tolerance and diversity, carry theoretical implications; philosophical, moral and legal directions towards which the practice of the profession is willing to move. The same can be said about community as a basic principle. When considering this argument, we need to realise that the principle of community is just as profound as the fundamental principles listed above.

In a society built on individualism, the driving force behind public thinking and behaviour is personal interest, the enforcement of which results in the intensification of competition, the narrowing down of communication, a deteriorating sense of solidarity, social discord and separation. In a community-based society, the interest of the community is given significance alongside individual endeavour. Community action undertaken by community groups for the sake of the common good is one of the main ways in which participatory democracy manifests itself. This process involves regular communication, participation and ensuing solidarity among community members. The social risk of neglecting communities is that the oppressed and marginalised become alienated from society in even greater numbers. If community is taken seriously as a fundamental principle of community development, we find ourselves on fertile soil because communities are sufficiently diverse to allow for the depth of community development interventions. Without this depth, the intervention remains mere 'technical assistance'.

The extent to which community development can contribute to the development of civil society depends on a given civil society's level of maturity as well as on the financial support available. The main problem, however, is that in Hungarian society there is a gap between, on the one hand, the democratic instincts of community development workers to encourage active citizenship and citizen participation and, on the other, the responsiveness of a society that is going through a slow democratisation process:

> Democratic initiatives that put people in the limelight demonstrate the risk factors of community action for the cautious, financially unstable, distrustful citizen. This can sometimes generate fear and even a kind of passive resistance. We feel that even now there is only limited scope for democratic initiatives. The reasons for this are complex, but I would point out that neither the educational system, nor adult education or our daily practice provides adequate preparation: they do not equip citizens for democratic participation. (Vercseg, 2005, p 402)

Hungarian community development is also being held back because of limited methodological developments. Practice theory, the theory abstracted from practice, involves new ways that are developed by practice on a regular basis. These are then summarised and analysed by community development research and included in new curricula and publications in a systematic way. If this process comes to a halt, the profession as a whole will suffer. We are trying to change a society that is resistant to our efforts; we are seeking to transform a power and authority-oriented culture into one that is based on the sharing of responsibility, participation and cooperation. Society is not yet willing to accept this approach and this has affected the profession. Social problems are so serious that we cannot handle or solve them by conventional means.

The roots of this problem are to be found in the social management policies enforced since the political transformation; none of them has sought to regenerate the injured tissues of communality and civil society, developing formerly non-existent functions and skills and strengthening social and civil participation as a whole. The measures taken so far have failed to renew or reproduce the social capital of the region in a more far-reaching and up-to-date manner. The development of civil society and the building and renewal of democracy would require the adaptation and development of new methods at the local level, as practised by community development and participation methods elsewhere.

The organisation of communication between local, regional, national and European civil institutions and networks is gaining importance. The following is an example of a national community development vocational network.

The Hungarian Vocational Network for Supporting Community Initiatives

This network started in 2004 as a result of the Budapest Declaration, with funding from the Ministry of Social Affairs and Labour. Since that time, a community development network has been developed in Budapest and the 19 counties of Hungary. The funding covers the practical implementation of local programmes and development schemes and the part-time employment of one community development professional per county.

The local development professionals look for active local individuals or existing community groups in a county's local communities. They provide consultations for them, organising the most active ones into local vocational workshops, training courses and exchanges of experience. They also involve them in the work of the National Vocational Network Development Workshop that organises national training workshops every year. A practice has emerged whereby community development professionals carry on working with community groups and issues activated earlier, often managing long-term community development processes. A minimum of 10-15 new local initiatives of this kind are organised in each county annually (Péterfi, 2008).

Due to the growing influence of the media, actions and campaigns can now play a more significant role in exerting influence on public opinion. For example:

Do it, you can!

Campaign for Citizenship and Democracy
Citizen Participation Week, 2008

Honorary patron of the event – Mrs. Kinga Göncz, Minister for Foreign Affairs

International head organiser and co-ordinator:
Central and Eastern European Citizens Network (www.ceecn.net)

Organisers in Hungary: Civil College Foundation
Hungarian Association for Community Development
Vocational Network for supporting Community Initiatives
Hungarian Institute for Culture and Art
Alliance for Developing Community Participation

Following the practice of earlier years, between 22–28 September 2008 hundreds of civil organisations have joined together to raise awareness on the importance of citizen participation and local action at a total of 152 local, sub-regional and regional events.

In 2008 the state of citizen participation in Hungary was put into the limelight, with reference to social capital. A total of 4100 questionnaires were collected by our volunteers. For the results and a list of local programmes, pictures, videos and reports, visit www.arh.blogol.hu. For press coverage, see www.arh.kozossegfejlesztes.hu. (Varga, 2008, p 13)

A UK perspective

How equipped is community development in the UK to work with communities facing challenges and opportunities? Is it too dependent on the ideas and practice of the past? Is it trapped in 'responsive mode' to the demands of the present? To what extent is it anticipating issues of the future – over the next 10 years and beyond? These are testing questions and we do not presume to set out comprehensive answers here. They are, appropriately, questions that are the stuff of group debates at conferences and workshops and within networks – arenas that bring together people from the diverse range of networks, organisations and institutions, something that is a characteristic of community development in the UK. Our contribution focuses on what we see as being the current policy, practice and professional challenges. Then, taking a forward-looking stance, we identify three key issues that community development has to address and that we discuss further in Chapter Eleven.

Current challenges

The *policy* context for community development is, on the face of things, remarkably buoyant. For most of the period from 1960 to 1990, community development enthusiasts working at the jurisdiction-wide level felt frustrated because neither ministers nor civil servants appeared to attach importance to community development. The scope for policy influence was minimal. Two of the most significant initiatives during this period illustrate the point:

- The launch of the Community Development Project (CDP) by the Home Office in 1968 was a false dawn. After a few years, the Home Office became increasingly anxious to distance itself from the local action supported by the 12 CDPs as well as from the radical findings emerging nationally. By 1975, influenced by several of the local authorities involved, it was clear that the government had decided to end the project.
- In theory, the position of the Young Volunteer Force Foundation provided an opportunity to open up the policy dimension of community development. Set up in 1968, its name was changed later to the Community Projects Foundation and then the Community Development Foundation (CDF). It is a non-departmental public body; its trustees are appointed by government and its operational plans have to be agreed with the relevant department, latterly the

Department for Communities and Local Government (DCLG), in order to obtain core funding. However, it was only during the 1990s that CDF began to exert influence at the policy level. Prior to that, it was essentially a fieldwork management organisation, drawing lessons for practice from the projects it ran.

The situation today is very different. All three main political parties embrace the ideas of localism and community involvement. The DCLG's 2006 White Paper, *Strong and prosperous communities* (DCLG, 2006b), encapsulated this commitment. However, Michael Pitchford echoes the thoughts of others concerning the preference for the terms 'community involvement', 'community empowerment' and 'community engagement' rather than 'community development':

> Colleagues have suggested to me that community development has arrived at the policy table. Interviews with experienced practitioners and observation of current practice suggests that it is the importance of 'community' to the New Labour government that has arrived and not that of community development. It is the newer categories of 'community engagement' and 'community empowerment' that underpin the 2006 White Paper and not that of community development. (Pitchford, 2008, p 93)

From April 2009, best value local authorities have had a 'duty to inform, consult and involve' local people in order that they can play a more active and influential role in how their areas develop. Since the White Paper, the DCLG has issued a series of further publications and guidance notes. Together they constitute an impressive commitment:

> Empowerment, under one name or another, has been an objective of social policy for several decades, but it has never had such a specific and high profile commitment in policy agendas as now. It is being promoted as a key concept in the way forward to a more healthy, inclusive and fully-functioning society, and is being included in policy developments applied to the whole population. (Longstaff, 2008, p viii)

Not surprisingly, national community development organisations such as CDF and the Community Development Exchange (CDX) have followed these developments closely. In general, they give them a guarded welcome, while at the same time emphasising the need for the new policy agenda to be rooted in community development values and principles. There is some anxiety that community development may be drawn so close to policy tables that its role of providing challenge and setting out alternatives will weaken. Those with long memories or who look at experiences outside the UK – that of Combat Poverty Agency in Ireland, for example – are concerned that community development organisations could suddenly lose favour with policymakers and be allowed to drift and flounder. Inevitably, much could change following the election of a new government in 2010.

Our assessment is that community development organisations have done well to be part of policy formulation processes. There can be no doubt of the importance of being close to the planning and decision making of state agencies because of the potential impact of their decisions on communities. Holding this position, however, is very testing for community development. It is too early to know if it has succeeded in managing the tension but the need to be aware of it, and being ready to handle it, is of profound importance.

The *practice* implications of the new policy agenda for community development were anticipated from the early 1990s by the increasing emphasis on the need for partnership working. Indeed, over the years, the cry of 'partnership' almost became a mantra for community development. In the eyes of some managers, the main purpose of community development was to service and facilitate the effective and efficient working of local and county-wide partnerships between statutory, voluntary, private sector and community organisations. Government gives considerable importance to the principle of partnership working. In England, local strategic partnerships have been established since the early 2000s and are seen as an essential part of neighbourhood renewal and other regeneration programmes.

The development of partnership working has not been restricted to the UK:

> The theme of partnership has resonated across the globe, whether the partners are different levels of government, business, NGOs, voluntary non-profit organisations, indigenous groups or community organisations. Government institutions are being encouraged to devolve decision making and promote participation through new forms of deliberative democracy and participatory planning which recognise the limitations of relying solely on the electoral process. (Taylor, 2003, p 31)

Partnership working, it can be assumed, is here to stay. Community development organisations have had to adjust to it. They can also, however, decide to question it and improve how it works. More significantly, they can make the case for ensuring that community development is not subsumed within partnership. This is the critical challenge facing community development practice. Can it square the circle of combining partnership working with grassroots action? At present, the balance is tilted too much in favour of the former. Community development needs to rediscover its commitment to working with local people in ways that maintain its independence. The case study of a project called the Kabin in East London highlights the extent to which bottom-up community development can be eroded:

> The case study affirms the local origins of the Kabin rooted
> in a bottom-up approach to community development, with
> evidence that as the project grew community development
> shifted towards a top-down approach, eroding organisational
> capacity to listen and respond with tenants to priorities
> articulated locally. (Turner, 2009, p 242)

Questioning the dominance of partnership over community development is not just the responsibility of national community development organisations. Practitioners themselves need to adopt a more critical stance, such as that taken by Sarah Banks, who advocates practice with a critical edge that takes the practitioner beyond his or her comfort zone. A local authority community development worker interviewed for research by Sarah Banks describes how the community development team in which she worked had developed a 'community engagement toolkit' alongside a training programme for use by councillors and officers wishing to undertake community consultation and work more participatively with local communities:

> While this was felt to be a positive development, encouraging
> better consultation and participation processes, there was
> also a fear that community development values would be
> diluted or forgotten as 'community engagement' becomes
> a management objective. (Banks, 2007, p 144)

One reason why the concept of community practice explored in *Critical community practice* (Butcher et al, 2007) is important is because it acknowledges the range of practitioners who, in one way or another, are involved with communities. There are regeneration officers, economic development staff, health visitors, youth workers, housing officers and many others who can contribute to processes that lead to the strengthening of communities. Their commitment to supporting grassroots work, alongside their involvement with partnership boards and other coordinating mechanisms, is as necessary as it is for community development workers.

Professionally, community development struggles to sustain the structures and organisations needed to ensure the effective delivery of good practice. The 2001–03 survey of community development workers undertaken by CDF and CDX found an occupation characterised by casualisation. The evidence showed low salaries, inconsistency among employers as to the level of experience and qualifications required for community development work and a rapid turnover of staff. Short-term contracts were widespread and there was considerable post insecurity for workers in the voluntary sector; even in the statutory sector, 30 per cent of the posts were 'fixed term' or 'casual'. The survey report contains some stark data and the authors point out that:

> Unless knowledgeable and skilled community development workers (paid and unpaid) are available to make contact with communities, win their trust and support their work, it is difficult to envisage programmes being able to achieve their community development objectives. (Glen et al, 2004, p 61)

The survey's findings on the role and scope of so-called unpaid community development workers were more encouraging. These are local people, most of whom have extensive experience of being involved with their communities. From the interviews with the survey's sample, it appeared that they were adopting roles typical of community development intervention and similar to those taken by paid workers. Two of the authors comment that:

> While being cautious about drawing firm conclusions from one small study, the unpaid workers study seems to show that, over the past 20 years, experience has been building in communities. Accordingly, there are now people who have acquired skills in areas traditionally seen as the domain of professional workers. (Henderson and Glen, 2006, p 282)

If the contribution of unpaid community development workers proves to be a strong trend, it will open up a significant new pool of resources – a throughput to the profession that comes directly out of the experiences of active and reflective members of community groups. The profession would become less dependent on the conventional higher education routes. This is the territory that has been supported for many years by the Federation for Community Development Learning and other organisations, using the national occupational standards for community development as a framework for working with local people who are determined to obtain qualifications through a choice of learning options. They can follow routes that can, if they wish, lead to certificate, diploma and degree qualifications. In Northern Ireland, the Rural Community Network, in its final report to the Carnegie Trust's rural community development project, reflects a growing awareness within urban as well as rural contexts when it states:

> With the decrease in the numbers of paid community development workers in rural Northern Ireland volunteer community activists will deliver the majority of rural community development over the next 20 years. The development of the skills and knowledge within these groups will be fundamental to the resilience of rural communities in Northern Ireland in the future. (Rural Community Network, 2009, p 47)

Sociologically, it is likely that the membership of the community development profession in the second decade of the 21st century will contrast in a number of respects with the membership in the 1970s. Then it was predominantly made up of university graduates, many of whom became involved in community development from having been active in radical student and peace movements. They were mainly middle class and did not come from deprived communities. Now the membership has drawn in people who have experienced community action and involvement. They are mainly working class and either live or have lived in hard-pressed neighbourhoods. There is a strong anti-racist strand in the changing profession. Given the increased importance given to higher education by governments and other institutions, and the expansion in the number of students, the new routes into community development could help to ensure that it stays rooted in the life and culture of local and identity communities.

The challenge facing the profession is whether it can sustain this trend and ensure that it is integrated fully with conventional higher education routes. What must be avoided is the emergence of a two-tier profession: on the one hand, graduates who enter community development directly from higher education and professional jobs and who are potential managers; on the other hand, entrants who have followed a less orthodox route and who may not be perceived by employers to be potential managers.

Two other points about maintaining the profession need emphasising. First is the importance of ensuring that there is a varied and critical community development literature. This is an essential component of a profession that, while experiencing uncertainty and problems in terms of membership, must be equipped to respond to issues and be prepared to invest time and energy in the development of theory. Second is the need to sustain the commitment to carrying out research on community action and community development practice and to making use of the research findings. It would be short-sighted to underestimate the influence that research evidence can have, particularly in the policy context.

Three issues

(i) Over the coming decade, the UK is going to have to act on a number of challenging issues. Some of these stem from the global economic recession that took hold in 2008; public spending will continue to be reined in and both unemployment and taxation will rise. Both of these will have an impact on communities, resulting in reduced services, deterioration of community facilities, increased poverty and social exclusion. Already there is public concern about the fragmentation of communities. David Utting reports that the consultation undertaken by the Joseph Rowntree Foundation in 2007 to consider fundamental questions about society and the problems facing it produced evidence of a 'pervasive level of anxiety' and that was a year prior to the onset of the economic recession:

> Widely shared ... were feelings of unease about the sheer pace of social change in recent years and concern that particular values relating to community cohesion and social responsibility have, somehow, been left behind. Whether talking about individualism, consumerism and greed, or about poverty, crime and drug misuse, there was a genuine sense of fear expressed in the face of complex national and international trends over which people felt they had no sense of control. (Utting, 2009, p 227)

Community development, like other professions, will have to gear itself to be able to respond effectively to these changes and challenges. Other issues also require sustained responses. We believe the clear priorities are the issues of diversity and sustainability.

(ii) In Chapter Seven we draw attention to the challenge of multiculturalism in the context of social control. The issue, however, goes well beyond this context and it is an issue with which the community development profession has to engage. There is widespread recognition of this. The question, however, is whether the profession is taking steps to equip itself so that it is able to provide effective responses. Not only must it aim to reflect the diversity of the UK population, it must also be in a position to work effectively with a variety of multicultural and faith communities. This requires the forging of strong alliances between white and black community development workers, enabling each to learn from the other. It also means being in a position to build confidence and trust between diverse communities, reaching out across apparent divides and encouraging dialogue and joint action. These imperatives assume that community development workers are sufficiently knowledgeable and skilled and it is here that there is an urgent need for critical reflection and learning.

(iii) A range of environmental organisations are campaigning to raise society's awareness and understanding of the likely impact on our lives of the combination of climate change and the critical depletion of energy resources. Community development organisations across Europe have sought to bring these challenging issues onto their agendas. Joint work between environmental and community development organisations is emerging. One has to question, however, the extent to which community development has taken the issue on board. Is it an example of an 'add-on' issue, one more topic to tackle?

Perhaps what is needed is proactive rather than responsive action allied to a willingness to be self-questioning. That was the approach taken by the Carnegie Trust's Commission for Rural Community Development programme. Between 2004 and 2009, it worked with local and national partner organisations across England, Scotland, Wales, Northern Ireland and Ireland. A number of these organisations had been set up to work on environmental issues, often using community arts activities to encourage debate and involvement. They provided a challenge to the community development organisations involved because of their commitment to environmental action and their capacity to mobilise people around environmental issues:

> The vibrant rural community of the future will adapt to
> the needs of a low carbon economy by reducing its carbon
> footprint, nurturing its biodiversity assets and reaping

the potential of community owned renewable energy generation. (Carnegie Commission for Rural Community Development, 2007, p 70)

Environmental action rooted in community development principles and methods cannot be restricted to the local context. It is grappling with global phenomena and in future we are likely to see more examples of local and international partnerships.

Commonalities and differences

The Hungarian and UK perspectives agree on:

*   the fragility of the community development profession;
*   the extent to which it is recognised by other professions;
*   arguments for locating resources for community development at community level, especially by providing opportunities for local people to become community development workers.

The historical and structural contexts of community development in Hungary and the UK contrast significantly. It is not surprising, therefore, that we can identify differences between the two perspectives presented:

*   The concept of civil society is inseparable from that of community development in Hungary and other countries in central and eastern Europe, whereas in the UK the connections are rarely made.
*   The community development profession in Hungary is independent from the state, whereas this is true of only a small part of the profession in the UK.
*   Community development in the UK engages with policymakers but this dimension has yet to emerge in Hungary.

In the following chapter we continue the comparison between the two countries in the context of training and learning.

TEN

Learning and support

What are the learning and support resources available to community development so that it is equipped to respond effectively to the challenges faced by communities today and in the future? Do community development organisations give sufficient attention to this question or are they so taken up dealing with organisational and funding crises that the question is not addressed with sufficient rigour?

Overall, the picture is a mixed one. There are some examples of innovatory systems and opportunities but also evidence of worrying gaps and failures. In this chapter, we use Hungarian and UK experiences to explore this territory, finishing with a European perspective and some general comments. The word 'resources' is used deliberately; our focus in what follows is on training but it is important to remember that training is only one dimension of resources for learning and support.

Hungary

There are the two issues that Hungarian community development professionals have been tackling through adult training initiatives: one is the development of a democratic and collective attitude, civil courage, skills and democratic techniques among citizens; the other is sustaining a democratic attitude and the willingness to be active in local political decision making and the economic sphere.

Civil College Foundation

Its experiences of democratic deficit led the Hungarian Association for Community Development (HACD) to recognise that the informal learning that takes place in community development processes must be complemented with formal learning. The association has developed an adult training strategy, organised into activities that focus on community, democracy, civil society, local media and community-based economic development. Northern College, the adult education college in the UK, provided considerable assistance in developing this system. The resulting community development training organisation, the Civil College Foundation (CCF), has become a national adult education organisation. It is a social organisation for public benefit. In 2003, it was recognised by the state as an accredited adult education institution.

Participants on courses are civil and community activists (often members of Roma groups, unemployed people and members of community groups from disadvantaged areas). With the help of the syllabus developed by CCF's 12 trainers and through participatory adult education methodology, they learn to think from their own community's point of view while at the same time acquiring civil action and other techniques. Most of the courses take place over a weekend. Field practice usually lasts five days; the professional course takes 120 hours overall. The number of participants on a course is usually between 14 and 32. Each year approximately 700–800 people enrol on CCF training courses.

When starting its operations, CCF received grants and donations that made it possible to open its residential training centre in a derelict school situated in a cluster of hamlets called Kunbábony. As well as hosting community activists from community development projects operating throughout the country, CCF has also played an active role in community development activities taking place in the surrounding region. Often it involves community development students in the regional development process and provides them with appropriate fieldwork opportunities. The organisation has frequently faced difficulties, ranging from the sheer struggle to survive to the issue of how far the college is capable of promoting community learning as a way of life. CCF places great emphasis on sharing experience and knowledge internationally. This is illustrated by the following example.

Thinking about democracy

This community-oriented democracy project was the result of a collaboration between CCF and Northern College, UK. During the course of the project, CCF translated five training modules developed in the UK and adapted them to the Hungarian context as part of a 'training the trainers' programme. The original modules were written by professionals at Northern College and the University of Leeds within the framework of a new learning programme developed by Adult Education for Citizenship and Democracy. The programme was organised by the Centre for Citizenship Learning and Activity, whose objective was to build up a network of adult training professionals, trade unions and voluntary/community organisations in order to promote participatory democracy. The modules highlight different aspects of democracy, building on the skills and experiences of users. The teaching of the modules has been integrated into the regular training activities of CCF (Grayson and Thorne, 1999, summary).

With the development of civil society, the expansion of its spheres of activity and the evolution of its networks, training demands at the national level have changed and increased. The emerging community and citizen activities, issues and problems required the development of a more sophisticated and diverse training system by CCF. This was made available in 2008.

The new system includes 25 training courses, all of which are connected to community development theory and practice and target the development of civil society and the strengthening of community involvement and community action. Twenty training programmes and curricula have been developed and used, and another five are being prepared. During 2008–09, CCF and its trainers ran four 'training the trainers' courses, six teaching workshops and 31 three-day courses. One explanation for the high number of courses is that, by using a number of fundraising channels, CCF has been able to reduce the price of courses.

A novelty of CCF's training courses is that participants can compile and build their own curriculum based on their needs. Each 24-hour course is considered to be a module. As a result of the internal credit system, those completing five such courses can apply for a basic examination towards a degree in community development.

CCF is also active in the following areas relating to training:

- *Network development:* in 2009, CCF started to build up a national adult training network for supporting community development, called Network for Supporting the Promotion of Regional Interests through Training. In its final form, the network will cover all the Hungarian regions; so far, network nodes are active in four regions. CCF is continuing its cooperation with the Vocational Network for Supporting Community Initiatives, a national community development network involving development workshops in every region and county of Hungary.

  These two networks play a decisive role in recruiting participants for CCF's courses. Participants are in day-to-day contact with community issues and community development processes in their respective spheres of operation. The network nodes and workshops also initiate their own activities. Individual candidates can apply for courses on CCF's website.

- *Local involvement:* with funding from different national and European sources, CCF has taken part in training the residents of the disadvantaged Upper-Kiskunság and Dunamellék sub-region either as a partner or as the main fundraising applicant for projects. The training centre also serves as a community centre for local people at no cost. Training courses organised for local people on a regular basis are also free.

- *Interdisciplinary summer camps* (in cooperation with HACD): each year, approximately 100–250 people attend these events, which are organised in CCF's residential training centre and the surrounding park. Participants come from different disciplines and exchange experiences on Hungarian and European civil society and community development.
- *Citizen participation week:* the 19 member states of the Central and Eastern European Citizens Network organise this annual event simultaneously with the purpose of bringing the issue of participation to the attention of the European media, politicians and civil society in a high-profile manner. In Hungary, there are more than 200 local events, involving more than 100 non-governmental organisations (NGOs); 4,000–7,000 questionnaires on public trust and participation are returned and there are over 50 media appearances.
- *Seminars and conferences*: CCF organises three to four national and international seminars, conferences or workshops each year. The foundation is a member of three international central and eastern European and Europe-wide networks (Central and Eastern European Citizens Network, Training and Learning Community Development Network and the Pan-European E-participation Network).

Those who attend CCF courses receive a certificate and an index containing the courses they have completed and the credits they have acquired. The trainers and CCF's managers are making increasing use of new online opportunities for communication and organisation and these are going to be integrated into an online course management environment (different online channels will be used – Wikipedia, blogs, databases, internet forums and so on). Efforts have been made to promote training courses. These include newspaper and radio commercials, promotional activities at professional events, banners and online advertisements, appearance on training-related web pages and mailing lists.

Figure 10.1: Range and phases of CCF's training courses

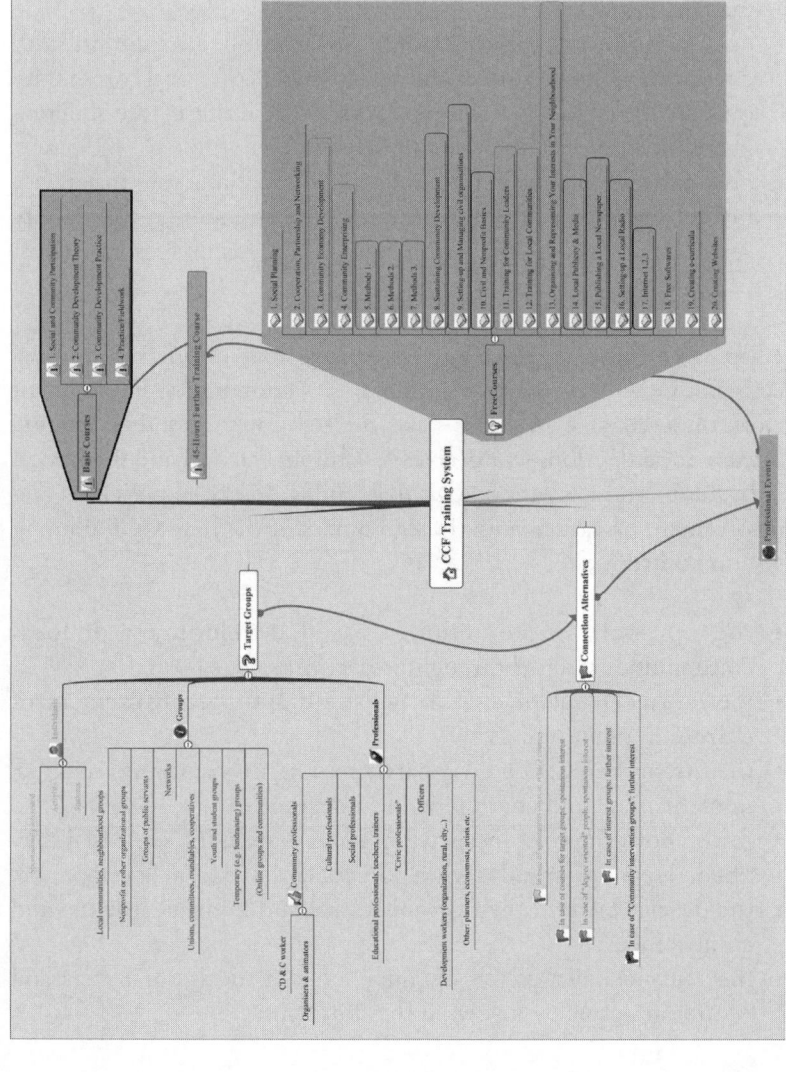

CCF's existence and the implementation of its objectives are extremely important because there is a serious shortage of adult training opportunities that:

- deal with community and democratic issues in a practical rather than an abstract way;
- cover not just the period of a project but also community development processes as a whole – members of a local community can attend up to five training courses that relate to the different phases of a given development process;
- give answers to the shortcomings of society in a way that is not market-oriented and provide training opportunities for community activists and NGOs in disadvantaged, mainly rural regions, at cost price or for free.

Apart from those cases where people join courses on an individual basis, CCF connects training with practical community development work undertaken with citizens and their communities, thus creating organic local development processes. With its practical and theoretical curriculum and a methodology that builds on the experiences and involvement of participants, the 25 courses of the new CCF training system contribute to:

- the renewal and community-based development of local communities reached through its networks;
- the enhancement of civil participation and the involvement of citizens in public affairs;
- the strengthening of civil participation in preparing, making, implementing and controlling local decisions;
- the empowerment of local civil organisations in the sense that they obtain recognition and take on potential roles in local development;
- the development of their organisational and human capacities and competence;
- the enhancement of the openness of local decision makers and economic actors by involving them in training.

CCF's training system targets the development of community and citizen action that is sustainable in the long term. The key elements for communities are a broadening of identity and thinking, development by the local community and openness towards universal values. The activities planned also contribute to the development of active citizenship, community planning/action and social involvement. These form the basis for the wide-ranging development of a more conscious and human-oriented way of thinking. The interlinking of community development and adult training allows activities to be adapted to actual local and social processes and ensures that the involvement of target groups is not undertaken on a temporary or short-term basis. The topics covered by the training courses assume a conscious and long-lasting commitment to local responsibilities through community development, participation, advocacy, civil organisation, partnership, local media, economic development and enterprise, digital literacy and the development of Hungarian democracy (Varga et al, 2008).

Hungarian Association for Community Development

While CCF is engaged primarily with training active community members, HACD emphasises the provision of vocational training for community development workers. The history of community development internationally tells us that the new discipline began to build up its own professional infrastructure (training system, professional literature, publications, standards, research programmes, advisory and other vocational networks) when the number of professionals employed reached the level of existing demand. This was also the case in Hungary, with the difference that, for a long period, community development could only satisfy the growing professional needs and demands for vocational courses within the framework of community or public education, the discipline that sponsored community development.

Accordingly, community development training courses were offered as an optional specialisation within community/public education higher-level courses, based either on the vocational course or integrated into further training courses for qualified professionals. This process has been going on since the end of the 1980s, creating various forms of community development courses involving different levels and durations. Over a period of time, this took place not only in community training but also on social work and rural development courses as well as courses targeting civil society and the not-for-profit sector. HACD and the Hungarian Institute for Culture (HIC), the institution providing the framework for the early experiments starting in the mid-1970s, have played a major role both in profiling community development and in organising the related training processes. The main Hungarian resources for the training courses included HACD's and HIC's research curriculum development and publishing activities as well as their international experience and systems of contacts, their community databases and websites, and two decades of experience in training and education.

Following its political transformation, Hungarian vocational training faced a set of new challenges, as did other parts of the newly forming Europe. In Hungarian vocational training, this involved a shift towards competence-based education and the renewal of the National Training Register, which means that outdated professions should be replaced by new, EU-recognised professions. At the same time, the standardisation of European training systems was also started in order to provide educational degrees that are mutually recognised in all EU member states. In accordance with the declaration signed by 29 European states in Bologna in 1999, the countries involved started educational reform processes in their respective educational systems, with an emphasis on establishing a multi-level training system: BA, MA and PhD courses that are interrelated and build on each other. In the process of transformation, new innovative training courses were introduced, including community development. The following community development training courses were initiated in this favourable atmosphere:

- The *community–civil organiser* training course. This is a state-accredited higher degree vocational course (four semesters). It is organised by higher education institutions and, although it does not provide a higher-level degree, it gives a higher-level vocational qualification in community and civil organisation and provides opportunities for further university education. Half of the obtainable credits (60) can be carried over by students and used on BA and MA courses. According to the preliminary information received, a total of 10–12 higher education institutions will introduce this state-subsidised course.
- The *community and civil studies* MA course. This was set up by the Department for Social Work and Social Policy at the ELTE University of Budapest and HACD in 2009. Following the accreditation process, the MA course is expected to be launched in September 2010.
- Higher education learning opportunities and the MA training courses are complemented by a postgraduate course developed by the Department for Social Work and Social Policy at the ELTE University of Budapest and HACD in 2007. This specialised further training, called *the community–civil development professional* course, covers three semesters.

The work achieved on training has resulted in the establishment of the Not-for-Profit Training Workshop (NPTW), formed by teaching professionals from 20 higher education institutions. The organisation and coordination relating to NPTW has been undertaken by HACD, with funding from the competent authorities. At the beginning, the workshop activities covered collective preparation and 'training the trainers' programmes, while later they included the sharing and evaluation of teaching experiences and meeting the requirements for launching the community–civil organiser course.

With regard to employment, a major shift is expected to take place, mainly as a result of EU programmes. In addition to programmes targeting the development of civil society, youth self-organisation, volunteering, rural micro-regions and the socioeconomic development of severely disadvantaged regions, a distinct community development programme is emerging. This means that important professional services can be made available to local communities in order to help their development succeed. These include training courses, the employment of community development professionals, advice and web development. In some programmes, up to 100 people may be trained and employed as community development workers. HACD has been a partner in planning these programmes since Hungary's accession to the EU in 2004. It welcomes the measures, but has concerns in relation to the processes planned for the future. There is uncertainty as to whether the programmes, which follow community development and European principles, will provide sufficient perspective for a discipline with a network of professionals expanding so suddenly. A question also being asked is 'Can these jobs remain sustainable in the future?'.

One problematic issue is that, in drawing on practical experience from western Europe, it is evident that most community development workers in the West link community development with struggles against poverty and social exclusion. Hungarian community development workers, however, have not been trained to have this perspective. Furthermore, community development in Hungary tends to attribute the social development potential of the discipline to facilitating civil and community education processes, not to tackling poverty directly. At the 2004 international conference at which the Budapest Declaration was agreed, it was striking that it was this issue that came close to dividing some western European organisations from their central and eastern European counterparts.

If grant-based initiatives become more widespread in future, community development professionals will have to decide how to make a living. There is anxiety that a servicing and business attitude in community development will become dominant in the region. HACD members are doing their best to counter this trend.

HACD is planning to launch a new national community/civil training movement. The idea behind it is for students to contribute to educational processes of communities and for older students to encourage younger people to become involved not only in their communities but also with the strengthening of democracy. It is hoped that the students' experiences will increase their commitment to democracy and to their community. Several of the conditions needed for organising the movement are in place:

- A number of civil society organisations are already teaching democratic skills, mostly with young people, and these organisations wish to cooperate.
- There are two national, informal training networks that also have an international background.
- National and international community development networks also wish to be involved.
- The Vocational Network for Supporting Community Initiatives has a wide-ranging system of contacts in all the counties. It is prepared to arrange hosting communities for the project in cooperation with the 11 national organisations and networks within the Alliance for Developing Community Participation.
- In relation to the NPTW's community and civil training courses run by HACD, students could have their involvement in the movement recognised as the practical field training element required by courses.

It can be seen that this challenging initiative is being taken up enthusiastically by potential contributors. It illustrates the positive position of HACD's training and learning work.

UK

There is no training and learning resource in the UK that is directly comparable to CCF's centre in Kunbábony. There are, however, local and regional resources that provide training and learning opportunities. These include colleges, regional groups of the Federation for Community Development Learning and national/regional community development organisations. The Scottish Community Development Centre is an example of the latter. It is a key resource for community development in Scotland, offering training courses, consultancy, information and policy analysis. Its position in Scotland demonstrates the extent to which training and learning opportunities vary considerably across Scotland, England, Wales and Northern Ireland – it is impossible to give an accurate picture for the UK as a whole. We can, however, generalise about trends and issues. Work has been undertaken on skills and knowledge for the Carnegie Commission on Rural Community Development (2004-09). One focus of the work was on the supply side of rural community development – courses offered by universities and colleges, community development organisations, independent trainers and consultants and community groups that provide learning opportunities. Evidence included urban as well as rural material. The main findings of the work point to a serious unevenness of provision:

> Community development always has to struggle to obtain and maintain recognition from policymakers and funding bodies and this is especially true within the context of training and learning. Inevitably, the focus on rural community development exacerbates this problem: it is perceived as being a minority interest within the community development sector and, in terms of its practice-theory and profile, it was a late starter. There is a sense that, unless attention is given to strengthening its position and modernising its content, the supply side of rural community development could become seriously weak and marginalised. The gaps and challenges are considerable. The position of rural community development learning within organisations and institutions is fragile. (Rural Action Research Programme, 2009, p 6)

Training and learning for community development at various levels has been available in the UK for more than 60 years and it is therefore concerning that the word 'fragile' is being used to describe the training situation in 2009. Key points that help to explain this situation have been identified by the England Standards Board (ESB) for Community Development Learning and Qualifications, the body that provides a professional system of endorsement of quality for all types of training and learning in England. The following reasons why community development programmes have failed in recent years are given in an ESB paper:

- The lack of Joint Negotiating Council (JNC) or other employer recognition which translates into the terms and conditions under which practitioners are employed (the JNC endorses youth and community workers' qualifications which have been approved by the Education and Standards Committee of the National Youth Agency). This has meant that course participants switch to youth work courses in their final year in order to have a JNC recognised qualification. Thus courses become unviable. We have spent a number of years trying to get the community and youth work JNC panel to recognise community development work endorsed courses. The JNC panel has consistently said that it no longer has jurisdiction over community development programmes. No other JNC or employer body accepts responsibility for community development.

- Many programmes are designed and piloted with project funding and they are unable to maintain themselves once the funding stream finished.
- Many universities and colleges have made their community development tutors redundant or redeployed them to other programmes where they can see a greater demand from potential participants.
- Many part-time community development courses struggled to attract enough participants in their initial years because of funding changes within higher education or insufficient support by employers to their staff to undertake part-time study (by providing time off work or help with fees). Thus people are left trying to juggle the demands of a course with work and home.
- There is a lack of consistency in employer demands or expectations for community development qualifications. Various surveys over the past few years have shown that few employers outside the JNC system for youth and community workers require their staff to have relevant community work qualifications; practitioners have a huge and varied array of degrees, diplomas and certificates. Many people have moved sideways into community development. Others have a primary qualification in another profession such as health or housing and are taking a community development approach to their work but without access to appropriate learning. This lack of demand affects many community development longer, accredited programmes. We have tried to provide guidance to employers about the different learning

and qualification programmes and why they should consider requiring their staff to demonstrate their skills and knowledge, but the sheer diversity of employers of community development practitioners, and of people who take a community development approach to their work, makes this a difficult task.

- There have been examples of experienced community development practitioners encouraging higher education institutions to develop appropriate programmes, working on a voluntary basis to achieve this. However, there is at least one example of the developed programme not then being offered due to insufficient demand by identified local 'catchment area' employers resulting in a 'business case' deemed not to be proved.
- The demands from many practitioners are for workshops, 'taster' and short courses, either non-accredited or at a higher level, but the recent government fee changes to master level modules have decreased people's interest in that as an option. (ESB, 2009, pp 2-3)

One of the problems faced by ESB is that institutions are not obliged to submit community development courses for professional endorsement – the motivation lies essentially with staff who wish to obtain recognition that they are running quality programmes. Some programmes, however, do not attach importance to endorsement because it is not linked to employment terms and conditions for students.

In recent years, funding to cover the costs of unpaid community development workers has been cut. There is also evidence of inadequate support (for example, for childcare, travel and learning support) to run introductory sessions for people coming into community development activity. Given the argument we have put forward that it is from this source that future 'cadres' of community development workers are most likely to come, it is crucial that this situation changes.

We noted in Chapter Nine that the work arising from the Carnegie Commission for Rural Community Development became increasingly focused on learning opportunities for members of community groups. Attention has also been drawn to the findings on unpaid community development workers in the 2003 UK survey of community development workers. The revision of the National Occupational Standards for Community Development, carried out in 2008–09, is important not only for the reaffirmation of key values and skills for the community development profession, but also as a means of reaching out to what appears to be an expanding constituency for the profession – members of community groups who wish to commit themselves to learning processes that will enable them to practise as paid community development workers.

This emerging, albeit uncertain, aspect of the community development learning situation provides an element of optimism for the UK training and learning context that in other respects is not buoyant. The earlier extract from ESB's paper on the situation in England captures some of the key issues and dilemmas facing training and learning in the UK as a whole. There are good-quality courses in some institutions, for example Goldsmiths College, London, the University of Gloucestershire and the University of Bangor, but overall the picture is one of instability and marginalisation. However dynamic and committed the drive to open up learning opportunities for members of community groups may be, the weakness of community development within the institutional training context must be a cause for concern.

A European perspective

The European dimension of training and learning for community development has become increasingly important. In 2005, the Combined European Bureau for Social Development (CEBSD) obtained funding under the EU's Grundtvig programme. The idea for a European cooperation and networking project arose from the Budapest conference (2004). Implementation of the project inspired a high level of interest from community development organisations across Europe. Partners in the project and participants in a thematic seminar demonstrated a high level of motivation to work together on community-based training, which is seen by many as a bridge between social, economic and cultural development. Community-based training can also make a substantial contribution to developing active citizenship and the skills of democratic dialogue that are so essential for meaningful participatory democracy.

The final report on the project provides detailed information on European community development organisations dealing with training. The Training and Learning for Community Development project (TLCD) was the first European-wide attempt to set out the principles of training and learning in community development and identify the community development and adult training organisations willing to engage in such cooperation:

In the light of the project, partners share the view that the experience of community-based learning combined with adaptability to diverse communities is the unique contribution that community development can bring to lifelong learning. (CDF/CEBSD, 2008, p 6)

The European Commission has sponsored the continuation of TLCD in the framework of its lifelong learning programme. CEBSD is the lead partner in a European project for dissemination of guidelines for training and learning. CEBSD leads a consortium for TLCD that consists of 16 partners who take an active part in exchanges and networking. They seek to apply the results of past and current actions in lifelong learning programmes to community-based training and learning. The partners are responsible for drawing the maximum benefit from the exchange of good practice and identifying the implications for European policy. The consortium seeks to exchange and share guidelines in order to:

• link core community development principles to training and learning systems that promote civic skills and community participation;
• set up an interactive network to promote community-based learning (with a focus on 25- to 64-year-olds who have not had third-level education) and link networking at the national level to the European level;
• increase networking from good practice to policy specifically in relation to the draft European guidelines for training and learning for community development developed in Budapest in 2006 under the EU's Grundtvig programme.

The consortium completed a series of exchanges where learning was relayed from partner to partner and country to country. The visits led to a laboratory in an old bus garage in Malmo, Sweden, being restored as an experimental community centre designed by local people. Here partners from across Europe analysed the most significant elements from the exchanges so far. Partners are now working on creative methods for networking and dissemination of results (Gorman, 2009).

Conclusion

In addressing the topic of learning and support for community development, we have focused on training opportunities for professional practitioners and local people. Most of the attention has been on qualifying courses. The material provided, however, particularly that from Hungary, alerts us to the need to engage with the training and learning agenda at several levels – at the post-experience and post-qualifying level, for example, as well as the qualifying level. The argument that the profession should adopt a strategic approach to learning and support is very strong. To place all the energy and resources in just one or two parts of the training and learning map will, in the end, be severely limiting. The following are especially important:

- The learning and support required by a range of other professionals who, in varying degrees, are making use of community development knowledge and skills need to be addressed. Both the Hungarian and UK perspectives refer to this category and it is integral to the concept of community practice (Butcher et al, 2007). There is the potential for grounding health, regeneration, rural development and other professionals within a clear community development framework, with far-reaching benefits for communities. There is also the potential to address the learning needs of managers and policymakers as well as practitioners and local people. Both of these are ambitious goals and they will take time to reach. The pay-offs, however, if the goals are reached, would be highly significant.
- Consultancy has tended to have a connotation of expensive contracts, with the work being undertaken by outside experts who cannot be held accountable by communities, groups and community development workers. In recent years, there has been evidence that community development has rejected this stereotype and developed an awareness of the benefits that consultancy can bring – targeted, tailor-made and up to date. This has been accompanied by the growth in the number of community development consultants, many of them former practitioners or trainers. There is, accordingly, a healthy equation between demand and supply. Consultancy can be particularly useful in providing support for community development projects.
- The Hungarian material refers to plans for developing learning and support on the web. A similar commitment has been made by the Carnegie UK Trust at the conclusion of its work on rural community development – a 'communities of practice' is being developed that

can provide opportunities for people to network, communicate, mentor and learn from each other. It will be achieved through a mixture of face-to-face events and a virtual network. Using the web in these ways will surely soon become part of the accepted landscape of community development.

This chapter reveals the parallels between the UK and Hungary in the search for learning and support. The themes can be traced, too, across the rest of Europe. Similar programmes have been developed and comparable tools and connections are being sought. There is no doubt that evidence of commonality could be traced if we extended the analysis to the global context. The ground-breaking handbooks for community development workers that were applied in Africa, *Training for transformation* (Hope and Timmel, 1995), illustrate the point powerfully. There has also been a striking growth of interest in training for research, especially participatory action research, a process that alternates continuously between inquiry and action, between practice and 'innovative thinking' (Hart, 2000). The method is now used widely in both northern and southern countries. Alan Barr has provided a European perspective on research and community development (Barr, 2005).

The dynamism of civil society organisations in struggles for democracy that have become increasingly evident across a wide range of societies will undoubtedly have needed to turn to good learning and support systems in order to sustain their effectiveness. There are also many examples of local groups and networks being both inspired and supported by organisations in different parts of the world. Different agendas connect with each other in the global context and networks such as those of the global civil society network Civicus and Call to Action against Poverty are clear signs of the need for learning and support to be accessible globally. Community development can learn a lot from civil society organisations in the global context about the benefits to be gained from sharing and exchanging learning and support experiences and tools.

ELEVEN

Conclusion

The previous chapters demonstrate the professional and community contributions of community development to building civil society. They also identify some significant challenges. These are the two areas on which we propose to focus in this chapter. Our purpose is to identify at a general level the contribution of community development to building civil society and to clarify the key challenges. We do this with the awareness that politically a shift to the Right is taking place in many European states and that, given the inherent political nature of both civil society and community development, this means that a high level of uncertainty will prevail. This is likely to be re-enforced by severe public expenditure cuts, caused by a combination of political changes and the impact of the global recession.

Yet the extent to which the importance of community development and community participation is recognised in both northern and southern countries is striking. Where the recognition comes from varies considerably, but in most cases the underlying commitment comes from communities themselves. The implication is that community development in the context of civil society is a high priority for societies. It is also clear that this connects powerfully with the concepts of social capital, equality and social justice.

The chapter moves between, on the one hand, anxiety concerning the fragility of community development and civil society and, on the other, confidence that their fundamental importance is widely understood. Towards the end of the chapter, we set out scenarios for the future of community development that reflect this ambivalence.

Contribution of community development to civil society

Community development is a very practical activity, for the community by the community. It is also a professional intervention. Community development workers need constantly to look for connection points through which people can act to improve the lives of themselves and others. They also need to draw on theoretical frameworks that can support professional intervention and provide a frame for self-reflection. Warren's fivefold typology can be used for both of these.

We have used the five functions in this volume as a means of focusing on key practice areas for community development. Readers will have noted that two of the functions – socialisation and social participation – are more significant in central and eastern Europe than they are in western Europe. Working on issues of economic wealth is mainstream for western community development but only emerging in central and eastern Europe. Social control and mutual support are under-developed throughout Europe. We have argued that in the central and eastern European context there is a need to deepen the roots of civil society and that, to date, community development has been able to make only a marginal contribution to this process. We have also, however, argued that there is a freshness and independent spirit within community development in that region from which western organisations and movements can learn.

The availability of new information technologies, communication opportunities and the politics of the European Union (EU) mean that the development of a supranational civil society is inevitable. Opportunities for mutual learning will increase. This means that community development has to gain confidence, improve contact building and organise within and across Europe-wide networks. What, however, will be the specific contribution of community development to building civil society? Can we, when reflecting on the preceding chapters, name this contribution and make it more tangible? To answer these questions, we return to the five ways in which, in Chapter Two, we suggested that community development could help communities to be part of civil society: challenging, defending, maintaining, recognising and strengthening. Do these remain valid and how do we recognise them?

Challenging: does community development still have a cutting edge? Is it positioned and ready to challenge the decisions of authorities? There is evidence that it does all of these. However, its style is more muted and less high profile than in the past. The explanation for this, across the whole of Europe, is that community groups are more locked into negotiating agreements with powerful agencies. The name of the game is partnership working and inevitably this places constraints on groups.

Yet most community groups have become more sophisticated in the tactics and strategies they adopt when challenging decisions or proposals. There is more recognition of the need for mediation between communities and organisations and a greater awareness of how conflict can be defused or resolved. The community development worker can play an important intermediary role, linking the local with more distant worlds and thereby opening up opportunities for community groups to challenge organisations and policies. This is vital when civil society is not being informed by strong and clear voices from the grassroots or where, in the western European context, civil society is dominated by large voluntary organisations.

Where community development workers support groups that take on the role of challenger they need to have a remit that legitimises that kind of work. This, it must be emphasised, is not because community development puts forward a case for special pleading to allow workers to support campaigning groups but because the capacity of groups to challenge is fundamental to democracy. Community development can help civil society retain the dimension of challenge, as can other interventions and social movements. The contributions that community development can bring are the experiences, learning and key messages of communities.

Defending: earlier chapters provide evidence of community development's capacity to be part of the response to defending key pillars of society's social infrastructure. It can be most effective in doing this when it combines its particular approach with that of others – in Chapter Two, we give the example of the Participation and the Practice of Rights Project. The work of Praxis, an organisation that takes a human rights-based approach to community development, is similar:

Praxis

Praxis was established in 1983 and is based in Tower Hamlets, east London. Its programmes include accessible services covering areas such as immigration, housing, homelessness, debt, education, benefits and health. It works with other organisations to provide healthcare services for those who are unable to access National Health Service provision and it also runs a service to support individuals to move into employment. It runs an interpreting service as well as working with a range of public sector professionals. Praxis uses transformative methods – for example, experience sharing, reflection, dialogue – with senior policymakers as well as practitioners and local people. It anticipates needing to respond increasingly to the impact on individuals and communities of global issues: war, the global recession and climate change. Praxis is committed to processes of reconciliation by bringing communities together in the creation of peaceful, multicultural neighbourhoods. Community development will continue to underpin all of the work Praxis does (www.praxis.org.uk).

Praxis illustrates how community development organisations need to be ready to change their approach and strategy in order to be effective in defending key aspects of civil society. Community development does not exist in a vacuum, unconnected to other social movements and organisations committed to building a strong civil society and to defending it when it is threatened. The implication is that community development has to learn not to cling on to well-established approaches, but to be ready to change direction in response to civil society's needs and opportunities.

Maintaining: the position of community development here is less clear-cut than the challenging and defending roles. In Chapter Two, we suggest that community development can help ensure the continuation of civil society, yet much of the evidence from the subsequent chapters underlines the danger of community development becoming trapped. This is because of the position it occupies now in many western European states in relation to the state; if it is not dependent on the state for funding and other resources, it is in danger of being pushed and pulled into either a subservient position (partnership working) or into service delivery. Both partnership working and supporting service delivery require community development to be adept at keeping a balance; involvement with partnerships can bring significant gains to communities and supporting service delivery can result in the reaching out to vulnerable groups. Too often, however, community development is being drawn into both these processes in ways that result in it being co-opted by powerful partnership boards or by demanding service delivery agencies. As a result, it is not in a position to help maintain civil society. It is not so much that it is being stopped or discouraged from playing this role, but that its identity has become blurred. As a consequence, it finds it difficult to be distinctive and thereby to be seen to contribute to maintaining civil society.

Recognising: community development's record on advocating the case for civil society has also been muted. The problem is partly one of resources; community development organisations do not have the staff to advocate on behalf of civil society. They are too tied into ensuring their organisation's survival. This, however, is not the only explanation for their minimal involvement in helping to ensure the recognition of civil society. They also tend to be:

• too isolated from other professions and interventions;
• insufficiently aware of the extent or magnitude of civil society. There is good understanding of the coalition between voluntary organisations and community groups – the voluntary and community sector – but less awareness of the depth of organisations and action groups in related fields, such as human rights and criminal justice;

- above all – in western Europe – too close to statutory agencies. Accordingly, they either fear the political and/or funding consequences of being seen to align themselves with campaigns to ensure the recognition of civil society or they are actively constrained from doing so. In the latter case, the judgement must be that they have been co-opted.

Strengthening: community development can contribute to the renewal of communities; the latter can renew themselves but sometimes they need intervention from the outside in order to become organised and to maximise participation. Renewed communities can take action on alienation, indifference, exclusion and damaged civil liberties. This, therefore, is the critical meeting point between community development and civil society. Civil society organisations have a decisive role to play in the renewal process because they can form coalitions of like-minded individuals and organisations committed to challenging and restricting aggressive power ambitions. They can put forward alternatives as to how society can be organised and they can encourage solidarity and cooperation. Community development is an essential cog in the wheel of these processes. Without it, the voices of communities will be severely weakened. In that sense, when focused on the strengthening of civil society, community development and civil society are inescapably intertwined.

One quality that an inspirational community development worker has is the capacity to encourage people with whom he or she is working to imagine a different future for their community. Often applied in step-by-step, unassuming ways, it is a quality that enables people to realise that 'things don't have to be this way ... we can bring about change'. The change process will be based on a vision of a 'better community' and it will be a community that forms part of a more dynamic and effective civil society. There are several ways in which this quality can be used:

- through informal conversations and friendship;
- by suggesting speakers who can describe action taken elsewhere;
- by arranging visits to other projects and encouraging exchanges of experiences;
- by taking group members through one of the many structured planning exercises that are available.

There is every reason to think that community development workers are delivering on this aspect of their craft, urging people to be ambitious in their thinking for the future. It forms a key part of community development's contribution to strengthening civil society.

Community development's capacity to challenge, defend, maintain, recognise and strengthen civil society relates to all of Warren's community functions. Inevitably, community development's contribution will be more relevant to some functions at a particular time than others and, as we have seen when comparing the UK and Hungary, there will be differences between countries.

The various players involved in community development – local people, community development workers, other practitioners, managers and policymakers – can identify and discuss the connections between the five ways in which we suggest that community development can contribute to strengthening civil society and each of Warren's five functions. We suggest that they can make use of the connections to ask the questions 'Where are we now?' and 'Where do we want to get to?'.

We turn now to three key areas of challenge that can be identified from the preceding chapters: the community development profession, communities themselves and civil society. All three are important, but, if asked to rank them, we would place them in ascending order of priority.

The profession

In earlier chapters, we identify the weak areas of the community development profession, notably the lack of resources for national and regional community development organisations and the fragility of European networks. In the western European context, we have also drawn attention to the unevenness of training provision and raised questions as to whether the throughput of trained community development workers will be sufficient to meet the continuing demands that are likely to be made on community development practice and policy. These are vital areas that need to be addressed. Given the pressures on public expenditure and organisational budgets, the difficulties of obtaining more resources to meet these challenges cannot be underestimated.

A very different challenge suggested by our material has to do with how the profession responds to new ideas and global issues. Will it cope with the lack of resources and the pressures of partnership working by turning in on itself? Will it have the energy to sustain regional, national and European membership organisations and networks? We pose these questions because it is hard to see where the space for thinking, debate, the taking of difficult decisions and negotiation between different understandings of community development is going to be found.

It is possible that advocates of, for example, community organising or asset-based community development will succeed in expanding these particular approaches. Our question, however, is about how the various advocates can speak and work with each other with the aim of sustaining one profession – a federation or network made up of different ideological, strategic and tactical perspectives that can act as one body. In the UK, the Community Development Exchange exists to play this role, but it cannot do so on its own. Responses to new ideas and global issues require a concerted and collective approach by a wide range of community development organisations, working closely with civil society organisations and movements.

Struggling to reach that goal is about more than idealism or consensus building. Rather, it is about having a profession that is united and strong enough to deal with issues that increasingly are happening in a global context. The threats to communities arising from climate change are becoming ever more evident. Participants in a workshop on healthy communities and a sustainable future at the 2004 European conference that agreed the Budapest Declaration were aware that they were responding to a major global issue. They committed themselves to the further exchange of ideas and methods. Were they, however, looking ahead to the long-term implications for community development of the issue they were addressing? We recall the workshop not to criticise its deliberations but to point to the real difficulty facing the community development profession of being able to absorb new and challenging ideas and evidence and reflect on their implications. The essential point is that the profession must remain open to new thinking and practice, be prepared to change its existing practice theory and forge links and alliances with new organisations and social movements. This is a tall order. It is a key challenge.

Communities

In the initial phase of community development in Hungary (second half of the 1970s), one of the novelties of the new discipline was that it raised issues of national identity within the neighbourhood and issues of locality or community identity within the country, in contrast to the internationalist ideology of state socialism. At a time when a centralised system dominated every aspect of life, community development attempted to legitimise decision making at a local level, linking it to local action, participation and control.

This reaffirmation, in very practical ways, of the importance of community is a helpful antidote to those who seek to dismiss attempts to define community or gauge its state of health. The Hungarian experience has been replicated countless times in a multiplicity of settings. That will continue. However difficult it is to state what it means, everyone needs community because it promises certainty, security and safety (Bauman, 2001). Both community development and civil society work on this premise. Accordingly, they always have to ask the questions, 'What is happening to communities?', 'What are their strengths and weaknesses?' and 'How can communities be supported?'.

It is dangerous to answer these questions in general terms because every community is unique. However, in the case studies and commentary provided in earlier chapters, we have touched on some themes that stand out. The impact on community life of security measures such as CCTV is certainly one of them. So, too, is the privatisation of large swathes of cities in the US and the UK – office blocks, expensive apartments and vast shopping malls patrolled by security staff that have been built cheek by jowl to neighbourhoods but are not accountable to communities (Minton, 2009). More familiar to community development workers are the themes of community decline, isolation and conflict.

It is essential that community development workers, researchers and others undertake this kind of exploration and analysis of communities. As people increasingly live their lives in a wider context, understanding community becomes even more necessary. The choices facing human beings and the influence on them of global factors re-enforce the necessity to have a community perspective. Furthermore, it is a normative perspective as well as a functional one:

> Lacking an approach to values ... free choice fails to make any sense ... since that sense is given by the existence of social norms, rules and frameworks. The social need for norms is what makes the role and need for communities so important in today's society. (Harkai, 2006, p 29)

Community development workers have to include this dimension of community in their practice in addition to functional dimensions. They need to work with local people on the question of why their community is important to them as well as on the question of how it can be improved – discussions about what is good or bad (values) as well as about plans and action (functions). This requirement tests community development workers enormously. Not only is analysing and understanding community extremely difficult but, so too, is working with local people on their beliefs and aspirations. Together they present a key challenge for community development.

Civil society

Civil society is a necessary condition for ensuring lively, strong democracy. In a democracy, opportunities for participation are inherent in civil society. As well as being key to local involvement, participatory democracy also has to build collaboration among the institutions, professions and sectors that are capable of influencing the development of participation.

In recent decades, following the changes of regime in central and eastern European states, South Africa and elsewhere, the number of states claiming to be democracies has multiplied. Whether all of them will survive is questionable. Civil society is the core factor that can sustain democracies and advocate civil liberties. The safeguarding of human dignity and equality before the law, equal opportunities, a tolerant society and the counter-balancing of powerful interests have mainly been the result of battles fought by civil society.

Yet in many parts of Europe, societies are learning that civil society is not always a synonym for a 'good society'. Those in power can often draw civil society organisations into being part of, or dependent on, their institutions and systems. As a result, civil society is weakened. We noted earlier how in central and eastern Europe most civil society organisations lack deep roots and a long, continuous history. Inevitably, this is going to mean that the process of democratisation will take time. There will be ups and downs, successes and failures. The director of the Trust for Civil Society in Central and Eastern Europe has warned against having too high hopes and expectations of non-governmental organisations (NGOs) in the short term:

> The last 20 years have brought indisputable evidence that in many areas such as human rights protection, rule of law, advocacy on behalf of disadvantaged groups, social services, development of new policies and practices and civic education NGOs have played a crucial role. But the work is far from accomplished. While most of the institutions and infrastructures are in place, the enormous task of making democracy work for all, and having human rights protection and the rule of law govern every aspect of life, still looks like a long-term project. (Gavrilova, 2009, p 37)

Community development interventions in central and eastern European countries have, to date, contributed only marginally to the process of ensuring that civil society becomes a lynchpin for democracy. This is said not to underestimate the achievements of the interventions, but to signal the extent of the challenge required to create a flourishing civil society.

The challenges facing civil society in the UK and other western European countries are different from those in central and eastern Europe because of the contrasting historical and contemporary contexts. We have seen how, in the UK, there is mounting anxiety about the negative opinions of political parties and representative democratic institutions; at the same time, there is concern that governments and their agencies have become too powerful, particularly when considering the extent of measures introduced to control citizens. Yet there are important parallels between the old and the new democracies with regard to the challenges facing civil society. In both there is:

• awareness of the need for the building and rebuilding of the independent basis of civil society;
• a realisation of the importance of addressing the democratic deficit as energetically outside the framework of constitutional reform as within it;
• criticism of localism and decentralisation policies that offer only tokenistic opportunities for influence and decision making by local people.

Civil society organisations face a formidable agenda. The critical issues are the capacity to respond to their possible loss of independence and the need to create more opportunities for participatory democracy.

Future scenarios for community development

A clear message emerging from the book's material is that community development currently faces in two directions. One way of expressing this would be to analyse the preference in UK policymaking for the terms 'community engagement' and 'community involvement', asking what the implications are for community development. However, an approach that connects more obviously with trends across Europe – even globally – will be more appropriate. We have chosen to use the terms *convergence* and *autonomy* to capture the two future scenarios mapped out for community development. We do this on the assumption that the community development profession and communities have a degree of choice over which scenario unfolds. A discussion that implies the inevitability of any one scenario would be irrelevant. Indeed, it would be alien to community development values and the conviction that change is always possible.

Convergence

We have seen how the language of community development, like that of democracy, can be picked up and used as common currency by a variety of organisations and institutions. This explains partly why community development is in danger of being turned into an approach that is highly generalised, merging with a raft of official consultation and participation schemes. The other explanation, however, lies in the realisation among economic development, planning, health and other agencies that they need to have ways of engaging with communities. As a result, community development workers have been drawn into supporting partnership boards and similar organisations. Increasingly, they are working on behalf of communities rather than directly with them. This trend was evident from a survey of community development workers in the UK. The authors of the survey report comment:

> For 35 per cent of respondents to state that they spend less than 25 per cent of their time in direct contact with communities might appear to some, at the very least, to be odd: is not face-to-face work with local people not meant to be the central part of a community development worker's job? (Glen et al, 2004, p 10)

The survey showed that workers were responsible for covering relatively large areas rather than one or two neighbourhoods. More significant, however, was the extent to which they were obliged to spend time in meetings and in report writing. This is worrying because there is a risk that practice will be distorted. There is widespread agreement that community development needs to work with organisations as well as with communities – the 2004 Budapest Declaration refers to the need to strengthen the capacity of institutions and agencies to work in dialogue with citizens – but this cannot be at the expense of support provided to community groups and networks.

It is likely that most community development workers have received only minimal training on how to work in and with organisations and coordinating bodies. It is an area of practice that requires a different set of skills to those needed for working with local people. Most workers will also receive limited management support. Perhaps, therefore, we should not be surprised if they become over-committed to partnership working. There are policy and funding pressures on them to operate at this level and, with rare exceptions, they are poorly equipped to operate there alongside their direct work with communities.

Two potentially positive features of the convergence scenario can be identified. There is, first, considerable scope for community development to be involved in interdisciplinary strategies, thereby increasing the spread of its principles and practice. Interdisciplinary team working forms an important aspect of critical community practice. Butcher and colleagues (2007) point out that this opens up a wide range of entry points to other professions such as social work, youth work, planning and regeneration. In a similar vein, a project being undertaken by the Homes and Communities Academy in the UK aims to increase the empowerment of local people as a result of the spread and improvement of empowerment skills among a variety of occupations. In the first report for the project, the professional ethos and training of five of the most 'empowerment-ready' occupations (planning, housing, police, police community support officers and neighbourhood management) are reviewed to reveal how far they incorporate community empowerment skills and remits. It also examines the extent to which community development is a key source for empowerment skills (Chanan and Miller, 2009).

Second, community development does not have to be diluted as a result of the increasing prominence given to community involvement and community engagement. Provided the latter are informed by community development principles, this area of work can bring significant results. In Scotland, community engagement is central to planning and regeneration. The 2003 Local Government in Scotland Act places a duty on local authorities to work together with public bodies and 'with such community bodies or persons as is appropriate' in developing a community plan. Guidance from the Scottish Executive emphasises the importance of ensuring that people and communities are genuinely engaged. It can be argued, accordingly, that community development, as a result of its underpinning of community engagement, has been mainstreamed in Scotland. This is an alternative to experiences elsewhere of community development tending to be marginalised by large programmes.

Autonomy

Independence has always been of critical importance in community development, encompassing:

- the freedom of community development workers to support groups that may make demands of local authorities and other agencies, even if the workers are employed by statutory organisations;
- the desirability of having a community development sector that is independent from statutory bodies; and
- the autonomous status of the community development profession.

We focus here on the last of these, albeit that the three are interconnected. A scenario of autonomy for community development would reflect a commitment to sustaining clear values, methods and skills. Of paramount importance would be a focus on bringing about change – or responding to it – with the action for change being driven from the grassroots. A continuing struggle to develop theories that explain and guide this approach is essential. Theories compete with each other, reflecting in part the diversity of communities, groups and organisations involved, but they can all be informed by common principles such as equality, diversity and cooperation. The 'best-case' scenario for an autonomous community development would include the following.

There would be an orientation towards *social movements* – locally, nationally and internationally – that are embedded in civil society. Inevitably, this will conflict with the employment situations of many community development workers; their managers will often question their role when they support campaigning community groups or when they appear to take the side of a group that is at odds with the local authority or other organisation. The community development profession has to struggle with this dilemma, not retreat from it. Furthermore, it needs to embrace the positive aspects of strengthening its links with social movements. Marjorie Mayo reminds us of the benefits for both activists and professionals arising from the sharing of local experiences in a global context via both the internet and face-to-face contact (Mayo, 2005, pp 113-31).

A return to community development's roots in *popular and community education* would be a priority. The influence of Freire's ideas continues to be widespread. Sometimes they do not form part of development and regeneration processes and they do not fit easily with a culture that is encouraged to focus on targets and outputs. However, opportunities can still be exploited for community development to cooperate with adult education, community education and the public education system. In general, these will be concerned with the democratic and community-based socialisation of communities. The UK government's White Paper for England on informal adult learning includes a commitment to invest in a support programme for learning champions (DIUS, 2009). A survey conducted by the National Institute for Adult Continuing Education found that there are 44 community learning champion schemes and about 1,000 champions operating in deprived areas. They themselves have had positive experiences of learning. They work at community level with the aim of encouraging hard-to-reach learners to try courses (www.communitylearningchampions.org.uk). There are overlaps here with the community development worker's role. The examples from Hungary given in earlier chapters demonstrated a high take-up rate from communities for courses coming from communities. Community development must continue its links with lifelong learning.

The autonomous scenario for the community development profession should include the element of being in a position to *deal with change*, to 'seize the moment.' By the latter we do not mean responding to short-term opportunities but rather having the capacity to analyse emerging themes and shifting paradigms with the purpose of understanding the implications for community development. Climate change and the global financial crisis present community development with obvious responsibilities to engage with issues of a new order. They are likely to require community development to test out new models of practice and to forge new alliances. Communities that already experience poverty and oppression will be exposed to a new array of problems. There are increased dangers of people within communities being set against each other as well as higher risks of conflict breaking out between communities. It is essential for community development to equip itself for these changes as well as to strengthen its global perspective. A combination of new initiatives with analysis and debate may be the best combination because this will help to ensure that ideas and dreams are tested and evaluated.

The litmus test for an autonomous community development profession will be to achieve *a balancing act*, the capacity to engage with policy issues at the same time as maintaining a commitment to working at the grassroots. This is a demanding goal, especially as community development needs to undertake policy work at local, regional, national and European levels. If, however, it is not pursued, an autonomous community development profession would undoubtedly weaken. It took a long time for the profession to commit itself to an approach that combines support for grassroots action, collaboration with large organisations and engagement with policy issues. It cannot afford to retreat from this framework.

Three overriding issues for the health of civil society that are very close to the values and purpose of community development are:

- mounting evidence of the alienation of many citizens from traditional political processes. Organisations that respond to this crisis tend to focus mostly on the need for constitutional reform. The attention is on the representative political system and there is a sense in which participatory approaches to revitalising democracy are seen by politicians and commentators as being, in comparison, a low priority. We believe that community development organisations should seize every opportunity to join with others in setting out the arguments for participatory democracy;
- the continuing existence of poverty and social exclusion among large numbers of Europe's population. This, combined with inequality of income and power, undermines the work of civil society organisations because a base line of human decency and possibilities for people to be part of an inclusive society does not exist. Community development organisations have a responsibility to join and support the work of anti-poverty organisations;
- manifestations of racism and xenophobia that are wholly alien to civil society. In the representative democratic system, the British National Party won two European seats in the 2009 election and the UK Independence Party has 13 seats. In communities experiencing oppression and poverty, the threat of attacks on members of black and minority ethnic groups has been heightened. The threat to civil society is clear.

Community development has to work with civil society organisations on these and other contemporary problems. It has also to engage with the long-term issues brought about by the global economic crisis and the implications of climate change. It must be ready to challenge how the profound concepts that inform and guide it – democracy, empowerment and participation – are being used. Last but not least, community development has to sustain its action with communities, helping them to present their opinions, demands and alternatives. This too fulfils a vital function for civil society.

This threefold agenda is formidable. It can be anticipated that, over a period of time, community development's performance on each of them will be uneven. It will also vary significantly in different countries. Yet if the pathway for the autonomous scenario is followed, the agenda can be addressed. Many community activists have experienced the joy of being part of successful campaigns and projects, often achieved against all the odds. On the wider canvas, we should also, during times of doubt and uncertainty, remind ourselves of the extent to which community development and civil society have won recognition globally. People's commitment to their communities stands out. Accordingly, they need community development to have an ambitious agenda. It is the solidity of the commitment that, in the end, will sustain the aspirations and energy of all those involved in the struggles of community development and civil society for improved and socially just communities.

References

Abrams, P., Abrams, S., Humphrey, R. and Snaith, R. (1989) *Neighbourhood care and social policy*, London: HMSO.

Advisory Group on Education for Citizenship and the Teaching of Democracy in Schools (1998) *Education for citizenship and the teaching of democracy in schools*, London: Qualifications and Curriculum Authority.

Andersson, H. (2007) 'Experience of working with participatory democracy in Sweden', *Parola*, vol 18, no 1-2, pp 41-3.

Armstrong, J. and Henderson, P. (1992) 'Putting the community into community care', *Community Development Journal*, vol 27, no 2, pp 189-92.

Arnstein, S. (1969) 'A ladder of participation', *Journal of the American Institute of Planners*, vol 35, no 4, pp 216-24.

Balloch, S. and Taylor, M. (2001) *Partnership working*, Bristol: The Policy Press.

Banks, S. (2007) 'Becoming critical: developing the community practitioner', in H. Butcher, S. Banks and P. Henderson with J. Robertson (eds) *Critical community practice*, Bristol: The Policy Press, pp 133-52.

Banks, S. and Shenton, F. (2001) 'Regenerating neighbourhoods: a critical look at the role of community capacity building', *Local Economy*, vol 16, no 4, pp 286-98.

Barr, A. (2005) 'The contribution of research to community development', *Community Development Journal*, vol 40, no 4, pp 453-8.

Barr, A. and Hashagen, S. (2000) *ABCD handbook. A framework for evaluating community development*, London: CDF Publications.

Barr, A., Drysdale, J. and Henderson, P. (1998) 'Realising the potential of community care – the role of community development', *Issues in Social Work Education*, vol 18, no 1, pp 26-46.

Barr, A., Stenhouse, C. and Henderson, P. (2001) *Caring communities: A challenge for social inclusion*, York: Joseph Rowntree Foundation.

Bauman, Z. (2001) *Community: Seeking safety in an insecure world*, Cambridge: Polity Press.

Béres, T. (2008) 'Micro credit and community development', *Parola*, vol 19, no 4, pp 11-15.

Blakey, H. (2005) *Participation ... why bother?*, Working Paper 2, Bradford: International Centre for Participation Studies, University of Bradford.

Bowles, M. (2008) *The community development challenge: Democracy*, London: CDF Publications.

Bulmer, M. (1987) *The social basis of community care*, London: Unwin Hyman.

Butcher, H. (2007) 'Power and empowerment: the foundation of critical community practice', in H. Butcher, S. Banks and P. Henderson with J. Robertson (eds) *Critical community practice*, Bristol: The Policy Press, pp 17–32.

Butcher, H., Banks, S. and Henderson, S. with Robertson, J. (2007) *Critical community practice*, Bristol: The Policy Press.

Campfens, H. (ed) (1997) *Community development around the world: Practice, theory, research, training*, Toronto: University of Toronto Press.

Cantle, T. (2001) *Community cohesion: A report of the independent review team*, London: Home Office.

Carnegie Commission for Rural Community Development (2007) *A charter for rural communities*, Dunfermline: Carnegie UK Trust.

CDF/CEBSD (Community Development Foundation/Combined European Bureau for Social Development) (2008) *Training and learning for community development in Europe*, London: CDF/CEBSD.

CEBSD/IACD/HACD (Combined European Bureau for Social Development/International Association for Community Development/Hungarian Association for Community Development) (2004) 'The Budapest Declaration. Building European civil society through community development' (www.cebsd.org).

CESAM (Centre for Community Development and Local Mobilisation) (1994) *Non-formal adult education in Sweden: A brief introduction to Swedish popular education – history, aims, ideology and economy*, Örebro: CESAM.

Chanan, G. and Miller, C. (2009) *Empowerment skills for all*, Leeds: Homes and Communities Agency Academy.

Chanan, G. and West, A. with Garratt, C. and Humm, J. (1999) *Regeneration and sustainable communities*, London: CDF Publications.

Cornwall, A. (2008) 'Unpacking "participation": models, meanings and practice', *Community Development Journal*, vol 43, no 3, pp 269–83.

Csányi, V. (2006) 'Humane to logical mechanisms of human communities', Paper presented at Hungarian Association for Community Development's Community Conference, Kunbábony, Hungary, 29 April.

Dahrendorf, R. (1997) *After 1989: Morals, revolution and civil society*, Basingstoke: Palgrave Macmillan.

Daly, S. with Howell, J. (2006) *For the common good? The changing role of civil society in the UK and Ireland*, Dunfermline: Carnegie UK Trust.

DCLG (Department for Communities and Local Government) (2006a) *The community development challenge*, London: DCLG.

DCLG (2006b) *Strong and prosperous communities*, London: DCLG.

DCLG (2007) *Making assets work: The Quirk review of community management and ownership of public assets*, London: DCLG.

DCLG (2008) *Communities in control: Real people, real power*, London: DCLG.

de Wit, C. (1997) 'The roots of CD work in the Netherlands', in H. Campfens (ed) *Community development around the world: Practice, theory, research, training*, Toronto: University of Toronto Press, pp 140-7.

DH (Department of Health) (2005) *Delivering race equality in mental health care*, London: DH.

DIUS (Department for Innovation, Universities and Skills) (2009) *The learning revolution*, London: DIUS.

DTA (Development Trusts Association) (2008) *Bearing fruit. Good practice in asset-based rural community development*, London: DTA.

Eade, D. (1997) *Capacity-building. An approach to people-centred development*, Oxford: Oxfam.

Edwards, M. (2004) *Civil society*, Cambridge: Polity Press.

ESB (England Standards Board) (2009) *Draft briefing paper on the professionalisation of community development*, Sheffield: ESB.

European Commission (1996) *Social and economic inclusion through regional development. The community economic development priority in European Structural Funds programmes in Great Britain*, Luxembourg: Office for Official Publications of the European Communities.

Flanagan, R. (2008) *Independent review of policing*, London: Home Office.

Freire, P. (1972) *Pedagogy of the oppressed*, Harmondsworth: Penguin Books.

Friedli, L. (2009) *Mental health, resilience and inequalities*, Copenhagen: World Health Organisation Regional Office for Europe.

Gavrilova, R. (2009) 'Moving beyond apathy', *Alliance Magazine*, vol 14, no 2, pp 37-8.

Gellner, E. (1994) *Conditions of liberty: Civil society and its rivals*, New York, NY: Allen Lane.

Gergely, A. (1991) *Institutional construction in local communities*, Budapest: Közösségfejlesztők Egyesülete.

Giddens, A. (1998) *The third way*, Cambridge: Polity Press.

Gilchrist, A. (2004) *The well-connected community*, Bristol: The Policy Press.

Glen, A., Henderson, P., Humm, J. and Meszaros, H. with Gaffney, M. (2004) *Survey of community development workers in the UK*, London: CDX/CDF Publications.

Gorman, M. (2009) 'Sowing the seeds of training and learning for community development' (http://tl4cd.wordpress.com).

Grayson, J. and Thorne, C. (1999) *Training the trainers, adult education for citizenship and democracy programme*, Budapest: Civil Kollégium Alapítvány.

Grigorova, D. and Georgiev, G. (2008) 'Supporting economic initiatives in Roma communities and the model of becoming an entrepreneur', *Parola*, vol 20, no 1, pp 1-5.

Harkai, N. (2006) *Community and community work*, Budapest: Közösségfejlesztők Egyesülete.

Harris, K. (2008) *Neighbouring and older people. An enfolding community?*, London: CDF Publications.

Hart, R. (1997) *Children's participation*, New York, NY: UNICEF.

Hart, S. (2000) *Thinking through teaching: A framework for enhancing participation and learning*, London: David Fulton.

Hautekeur, G. (2005) 'Community development in Europe', *Community Development Journal*, vol 40, no 4, pp 385-98.

Havas, P. and Varga, A. (2006) *From environmental education to the pedagogical practice of sustainability*, Budapest: Országos Közoktatási Intézet.

Henderson, P. (2001) 'Doing with, not doing for', *Mental Health Today*, November, pp 22-4.

Henderson, P. (2005) *Including the excluded: From practice to policy in European community development*, Bristol: The Policy Press.

Henderson, P. (2008) 'Community development: historical overview', in M. Pitchford (ed) *Making spaces for community development*, Bristol: The Policy Press (in association with Community Development Foundation), pp 7-15.

Henderson, P. and del Tufo, S. (1991) *Community work and the probation service*, London: HMSO.

Henderson, P. and Glen, A. (2006) 'From recognition to support: community development workers in the United Kingdom', *Community Development Journal*, vol 41, no 3, pp 277-92.

Henderson, P. and Thomas, D.N. (2002) *Skills in neighbourhood work* (3rd edn), London: Routledge.

Hill, M. (2007) 'The role of communities in care', in S. Balloch and M. Hill (eds) *Care, community and citizenship*, Bristol: The Policy Press, pp 5-19.

Hirsch, D. (2005) *Facing the cost of long-term care: Meeting the challenges of ageing in the 21st century*, London: Department for Work and Pensions.

HM Government (2009) *Hate crime – the cross-government action plan*, London: HM Government.

HM Treasury (2002) *The role of the voluntary and community sector in service delivery: A cross-cutting review*, London: HM Treasury.

Home Office (2004) *Building communities, beating crime*, London: HMSO.

Hope, A. and Timmel, S. (1995) *Training for transformation*, London: ITDG Publishing.

Hunti, M. and Halmai, Z. (2008) 'Reflex social co-operative', *Parola*, vol 19, no 4, pp 19-20.

Huszár, T. (1975) *The acting human*, Budapest: Szépirodalmi Könyvkiadó.

Jacobs, J. (1961) *The death and life of the great American cities*, New York, NY: Random House and Vintage Books.

Jensen, J. and Miszlivetz, F. (2003) *The languages of civil society and beyond*, CISONET Draft Report, Szombathely: Institute for Social and European Studies.

Keane, J. (1998) *Civil society: Old images, new visions*, Cambridge: Polity Press.

Keane, J. (2003) *Global civil society?*, Cambridge: Cambridge University Press.

Kovács, L. (2007) 'Teaching local history. A conception, 1994-2000', Mimeo, Szegvár: Szegvár Secondary School.

Kramer, R.M. and Specht, H. (eds) (1969) *Readings in community organisation practice*, Englewood Cliffs, NJ: Prentice-Hall.

Kraushaar, R., Hibbard, M. and Wells, B. (1999) 'Editorial introduction: community development in the United States', *Community Development Journal*, vol 34, no 1, pp 1-3.

Kretzmann, J.P. and McKnight, J.L. (1993) *Building communities from the inside out: A path toward finding and mobilising a community's assets*, Chicago, IL: ACTA Publications.

Kundnani, A. (2009) *Spooked! How not to prevent violent extremism*, London: Institute of Race Relations.

Kuti, É. (1998) *Let's call it not-for-profit*, Budapest: Nonprofit Kutatócsoport.

Lloyd, L. and Gilchrist, A. (1994) 'Community caremongering – principles and paradoxes', *Care in Place*, vol 1, no 2, pp 133-44.

Longstaff, B. (2008) *The community development challenge: Strategies*, London: CDF Publications.

MacAulay, S. (2001) 'The community economic development tradition in Eastern Nova Scotia, Canada: ideological continuities and discontinuities between the Antigonish movement and the family', *Community Development Journal*, vol 16, no 2, pp 111-21.

Matějů, P. (2004) 'Trust and reciprocity networks: two distinctive dimensions of social capital', *Parola*, vol 15, no 3, pp 8-9.

Mathie, A. (2006) 'Who is driving development? ABCD and its potential to deliver on social justice', in International Association for Community Development (IACD) (ed) *Does asset-based community development deliver social justice?*, Falkland: IACD, pp 2-5.

Mayo, M. (2005) *Global citizens*, London: Zed Books.

Mayo, M. (2006) 'Remarks from the chair', in International Association for Community Development (IACD) (ed) *Does asset-based community development deliver social justice?*, Falkland: IACD, p 1.

Mayo, M. and Taylor, M. (2001) 'Partnerships and power in community regeneration', in S. Balloch and M. Taylor (eds) *Partnership working. Policy and practice*, Bristol: The Policy Press, pp 39-56.

Mészáros, Zs. (1999) *The developing economic culture programme*, Report to Soros Foundation: Kunszentmiklós.

Mészáros, Zs. and Vercseg, I. (2006) *The state of human resources in the Upper Kiskunság region*, Kunadacs: Felső Kiskunsági Közösségi Munkások Egyesülete.

Miller, S.M., Rein, M. and Levitt, R. (1995) 'Community action in the United States', in G. Craig and M. Mayo (eds) *Community empowerment*, London: Zed Books, pp 112-26.

Minton, A. (2008) 'Why are fear and distrust spiralling in 21st century Britain?', *Viewpoint*, York: Joseph Rowntree Foundation.

Minton, A. (2009) *Ground control*, London: Penguin Books.

Miszlivetz, F. (1999) '"Civic or civil society?" Hungarian Television channel 2, 23 March', in F. Csefkó and Cs. Horváth (eds) *Hungarian and European civil society*, Pécs: Friedrich Ebert Stiftung, pp 423-34.

Oborne, P. and Jones, J. (2008) *Muslims under siege: Alienating vulnerable communities*, Wivenhoe: Democratic Audit, Human Rights Centre, University of Essex.

O'Leary, T. (2006) *Asset-based approaches to rural community development: A literature review and resources*, Falkland: International Association for Community Development (for Carnegie UK Trust).

Pahl, R. (1995) 'Friendly society', *New Statesman & Society*, 10 March, p 20.

Paksi, B. and Schmidt, A. (2006) *The mental health of teachers with special regard to the dimensions influencing the passing on of values in school, health improvement and problem handling*, Budapest: Országos Közoktatási Intézet.

Pearce, J. (2000) 'Development, NGOs, and civil society', in D. Eade (ed) *Development, NGOs, and civil society*, Oxford: Oxfam, pp 15-43.

Péterfi, F. (2008) 'Vocational network for supporting community initiatives', *Parola*, vol 19, no 1, pp 1-10.

Péterfi, F. (2009) 'Advocacy, interest promotion and power control', *Civil Review*, vol 6, no 1-2, pp 78-94.

Pitchford, M. (2008) *Making spaces for community development*, Bristol: The Policy Press (in association with Community Development Foundation).

Power Inquiry (2006) *Power to the people*, York: Joseph Rowntree Charitable Trust and Joseph Rowntree Reform Trust.

Purdue, D. (ed) (2007) *Civil societies and social movements: Potential and problems*, Abingdon: Routledge.

Putnam, R. (1993) 'The prosperous community – social capital and public life', *The American Prospect*, vol 13, no 4, pp 27-40.

Putnam, R. (2000) *Bowling alone: The collapse and revival of American community*, New York, NY: Simon & Schuster.

Quilgars, D. (2002) *Communities caring and developing: Lessons from Hull*, York: Centre for Housing Policy, University of York.

Rorty, R. (1989) *Contingency, irony, and solidarity*, Cambridge: Cambridge University Press.

Ross, M. (1955) *Community organisation: Theory, principles and practice*, New York, NY: Harper and Row.

Rural Action Research Programme (2009) *The supply side of rural community development*, Dunfermline: Carnegie UK Trust.

Rural Community Network (2009) *Community activism in a changing rural context*, Cookstown: Rural Community Network.

Schoenberg, S. (1979) 'Criteria for evaluation of neighbourhood viability in working-class and poor areas in core cities', *Social Problems*, vol 27, no 1, pp 69-78.

Schuringa, L. (2005) *Community work and Roma inclusion*, Utrecht: Spolu International Foundation.

Scurfield, L. (2009) 'Women, prisons and health – assessing the situation in Europe', in *Around Europe*, Brussels: Quaker Council for European Affairs, no 308, pp 1 & 4.

Seckinelgin, H. (2002) *Civil society as a metaphor for western liberalism*, London: Centre for Civil Society, London School of Economics.

Seebohm, P. and Gilchrist, A. (2008) *Connect and include: An exploratory study of community development and mental health*, London: National Social Inclusion Programme (in association with Community Development Foundation).

Seebohm, P., Henderson, P., Munn-Giddings, C., Thomas, P. and Yasmeen, S. (2005) *Together we will change: Community development, mental health and diversity*, London: The Sainsbury Centre for Mental Health.

Sharkey, P. (2000) 'Community work and community care: links in practice and education', *Social Work Education*, vol 19, no 1, pp 8-17.

Skinner, S. (2006) *Strengthening communities. A guide to capacity building for communities and the public sector*, London: CDF Publications.

Spratt, E. and James, J. (2008) *Faith, cohesion and community development*, London: CDF Publications.

Steele, T. (2007) *Knowledge is power: The rise and fall of European education movements 1848–1939*, Oxford: Peter Lang.

Taylor, M. (2003) *Public policy in the community*, Basingstoke: Palgrave Macmillan.

Turner, A. (2009) 'Bottom-up community development: reality or rhetoric? The example of the Kingsmead Kabin in East London', *Community Development Journal*, vol 44, no 2, pp 230-47.

Utting, D. (2009) 'Afterword', in D. Utting (ed) *Contemporary social evils*, Bristol: The Policy Press for the Joseph Rowntree Foundation, pp 225-31.

Varga, A.T. (1975) 'The functional system of cultural centres', *Kultúra és közösség*, vol 2, no 4, p 33.

Varga, A.T. and Vercseg, I. (1998) *Community development*, Budapest: Magyar Művelődési Intézet.

Varga, M. (2008) 'Citizens Participation Week results 2008', *Parola*, vol 19, no 3, p 13.

Varga, Máté, Benedek, G., Bodorkós, B., Giczey, P., Gyenes, Zs., Kovács, E., Mészáros, Zs., Peták, P., Péterfi, F., Pósfay, P., Varga, Matild and Vercseg, I. (2008) *The new training system of the Civil College Foundation*, Budapest: Civil Kollégium Alapítvány.

Vercseg, I. (1999) *Civil society, citizenry and community development*, Budapest: Közösségfejlesztők Egyesülete.

Vercseg, I. (2004) 'Measuring social capital in Hungarian local communities', *Parola*, vol 15, no 3, pp 10-15.

Vercseg, I. (2005) 'Central and eastern Europe in the limelight', *Community Development Journal*, vol 40, no 4, pp 399-404.

Waite, M. (2009) *Combining diversity with common citizenship*, York: Joseph Rowntree Charitable Trust.

Walker, R. and Craig, G. (2009) *Community development workers for BME mental health: Embedding sustainable change*, Report to the National Institute for Mental Health in England national workforce programme and the Department of Health Programme for delivering race equality in mental healthcare, York: Elliott Walker Consultancy.

Warren, R. (1963) *The community in America*, Chicago, IL: Rand McNally.

Wilkinson, R. and Pickett, K. (2009) *The spirit level: Why more equal societies almost always do better*, London: Penguin Books.

Wilks-Heeg, S. (2008) 'The canary in a coalmine? Explaining the emergence of the British National Party in English local politics', *Parliamentary Affairs*, November, pp 1–22.

Woolcock, M. (2001) 'The place of social capital in understanding social and economic outcomes', *ISUMA Canadian Journal of Policy Research*, vol 20, no 1, pp 11–17.

Index

A

Aarhus Convention (1998) 117
Abrams, Philip 120
'accelerator institutions' 92
active citizenship 137
  and community-based learning 46,
    48, 51-2, 170
'active community schools' in
  Romania 53-4
adult education 57-9, 187-8
  and community development
    learning 57, 151-2
    Civil College Foundation (CCF)
      (Civil Kollégium Alapítvány) in
      Hungary 157-63
  community education in central and
    eastern Europe 37, 38-40, 53-4
  popular education in Scandinavia
    55-6, 58, 59
  see also training
Adult Education for Citizenship and
  Democracy (UK) 158
Advisory Group on Education for
  Citizenship and the Teaching of
  Democracy in Schools (UK) 52
advocacy
  community development and civil
    society 178-9
  in Hungary 115-17
agricultural initiatives 66
  see also rural community
    development work
Agro-Information Centre in Bulgaria
  66
Alinsky, Saul 23, 34
America *see* North America; United
  States
Amnesty International 116
anomie and norm-forming role of
  communities 114-15
anti-poverty work 94, 189
Antigonish Movement 41
Armstrong, J. 122
Arnstein, Shelley 86
asset-based community development
  41, 63-4, 74-7, 181
  critique and demands of 75-7

associational life
  and civil society 11, 12, 17-18
    in central and eastern Europe 13,
      146
Autonomy Foundation (AF)
  (Autonómia Alapítvány)
  (Hungary) 66-8, 126
autonomy scenario 184-5, 187-9

B

Bangladesh: Grameen Bank 64
banking and community development
  64
Banks, Sarah 79-80, 150
Barr, Alan 80, 122, 133, 173
'bee work' in Hungary 89
belonging and participation 84, 89
black and minority ethnic (BME)
  groups
  and mental health services 123-5,
    127
  see also race issues and xenophobia
Blakey, H. 125
BNP *see* British National Party
  (BNP)
bonding social capital 88, 112
Bowles, M. 87
Bradford *see* Sharing Voices Bradford
  (SVB)
bridging social capital 88, 112-13
British Citizenship Survey 88
British National Party (BNP) 24,
  103-4, 189
Budapest Declaration (2004) 137,
  139, 140-1, 145, 165, 170, 181, 185
Building communities, beating crime
  (White Paper) 100
Bulgaria 65, 66
businesses: community businesses 62,
  63
Butcher, Hugh 78, 150-1, 186

C

Call to Action against Poverty 173